Paradise by Candlelight

by Susan Dunn Cobb

Paradise by Candlelight

Copyright © 2016

Susan Dunn Cobb

Revised 9/18/2016

paradisebycandlelight.wordpress.com

Dedicated to Glenn

and all of the fatherless

Table of Contents

Foreword

Who are you and why are you here? The questions remain after all talents, gifts, possessions, and loved ones have been stripped away, and we find ourselves standing alone in the universe.

When I read history, it is apparent every generation is provided with a test. Life, always a series of tests, appears to honor some lives more. These discover while they may be actors on a world's stage, they must perform under extreme difficulty. My hope is to soften your judgments toward the members of the cast on this particular stage.

Journey back through time with me for a moment. I have often thought what I would have done if I had lived when:

Christians would be thrown to the lions, and I watched my friends and neighbors rounded up and taken.

The Inquisition would cause the wealthy landowners to disappear, but poverty was keeping my salvation and earthly existence intact. The church preached they were the only way to heaven but they were giving advance tickets to the wealthy by way of torture and death.

After a long and arduous journey to the new world of America, my friends and neighbors would be butchered by savages. As a young pioneer with a family I would need to re-evaluate the cost of maintaining pacifist, Quaker beliefs.

English soldiers would demand to stay in my home and then terrorized my family. I would face the treasonous choice of becoming a Tory knowing my best friend and neighbor would remain a loyal Whig. The church I belonged to would continue to preach allegiance to the crown, saying it would fulfill the requirements of the Scripture to "obey all those who have authority over you".

I would witness slaves mistreated, separated from families, and killed, but our family slaves were my nannies, cooks, and playmates. My parents taught all people were not created equal, but some were to be regarded as material wealth and possessions.

Hitler would take over Germany and began systematic genocide of a large group of law-abiding citizens. I would have some ability to save Jews, the disabled, and blacks by hiding them in my home. As a good Christian I would want to do something, but if I chose to do anything on their behalf I would risk their same fate.

Drugs would invade a nation like cancer, but a large consensus of the population believed the law and the police were meddling with free will choices of peaceful citizens. Then drugs destroyed a member of the family.

Four days after the birth of a fourth child I would become a victim of domestic abuse and forced into years of hiding, just another crime statistic. The brain damage received would leave an insidious disability, but the children, nevertheless, required care. After struggling alone for a few years, marriage to another disabled person would help heal the trauma. Housing would become unavailable, yet my husband and I would maintain minimum wage jobs while staying in tents, vehicles, and trailers. We would discover homeless existence was a personal threat to those living around us, and now as a hunted refugee for the crime of poverty I would watch my children assaulted by the wrath of a whole city.

The last scenario is my story, and I share the way our family chose to meet our Goliath.

We are all alike in that we cannot escape pain, suffering, or death; but the way we live our life defines who we are. When the Apostle Paul said, "I have learned to be content in whatsoever state I am", he was in the state of being in prison and with no remorse for the activities responsible for landing him there. He was not bound by circumstances. They did not define him. He was completely free to do everything God told him. As it turned out, Paul wrote most of the New Testament, and much of this during his prison time. Apparently, our stations in life do not necessarily determine what we accomplish. Neither do they measure our value with the Almighty. Consider where he put his own child.

Where has God placed you in life? Is it close to the manger? If so, then thank him for the honor and keep your eyes open. You have words of life and hope to give to an important person who will soon be brought into your life. You might even get to bring them into your bus.

And we know that all things work together for good to them that love God, to them who are called according to his purpose.

Romans 8:28 King James Version Holy Bible

Freedom

They watched, as the little boy was slammed against the bow of the old, wooden, cabin cruiser. Almost he'd been tossed over the rail, but once again the screaming toddler fell back into the churning sea. They watched from their nearby perches on the rolling deck of the leaking, old, fishing boat.

A half-mile away in Santa Barbara free harbor many boats danced happily against their tethers. The mid-afternoon winds were whipping up the waves into a frothy green shake as the warm sun beat down on the backs of the deeply tanned men of the sea. The short, stocky owner of the vessel kept a close eye on the Weber hanging off the bow where it had been attached securely. Two thin, stainless steel arms served their purpose well by keeping any chance of a stray coal from rolling onto the deck and igniting the wood of the rickety boat. Whiffs of hickory and cayenne wafted up from the perfectly cooked chicken and wrapped around the weathered men, enticing them with the swirling mixture. Sea air salted the aroma, and patiently they ignored the growling sounds of their stomachs.

They watched the thrashing of the nearby souls struggling against the choppy sea current—the valiant attempts of two men to get the toddler out of the water and onto the deck of the decaying cruiser. When the dinghy first approached to starboard the older man had not waited for the younger to finish tying up. In the attempt to hoist himself over the wooden railing of the Tabitha the dinghy disappeared. It had sunk with the speed of the quick wave sneaking up behind like an unseen fist, smashing it down to secret places deep below.

Through the binoculars the scrawny, long-haired man watched, while at the other boat, a broad-shouldered, dark-haired man in a faded Hawaiian shirt grasped at the rail and held on with two fingers. Waves, body-slamming him as though they had caught him in a watery mosh pit, tried their best to fling him off. He not only hung on but managed to pull himself onto the deck, and he stood there looking like a rag doll after having been shaken in a dog's mouth. Below him, the young man thrashed about struggling to stay near the boat. He fought against the current carrying away out to sea the little guy he had barely managed to snatch.

They saw it all when the attempt was made to throw the kid aboard. The second time the small body smacked hard into the unforgiving wood. The well-built young man caught him as he fell into the water and with his long arms tossed him behind and onto his back. Short little arms choked the neck of the one who was keeping the swirling green mass from swallowing the tasty morsel. In a moment, the child was plucked off the back by those same arms for another attempt. Kicking and squalling, the terrified youngster grasped at the air while the young man submerged briefly to push the kid higher.

The older man leaned over the rail, snatching at the child while the waves teased and dipped whenever the father got close. Finally, as though the sea were tired of the game, the water-soaked man managed to grab a flailing wrist and flung the boy up over the rail, clutching him close to his chest. Small arms again choked the neck of this rescuer, and his little back heaved with sobs as he buried his head under the protection of the man's arms. The salt from sea spray mixed with the father's tears, itching and irritating the man's face. He swiped the back of his wet arm across his eyes while hugging his baby next to him. A wave crested, lifting the remaining son in a better position for the man to grab, and leaning over he was able to catch a hand and bring it to the rail. Quickly, he lifted himself up and over.

Stripping off the clothes and soggy life jacket, the father cradled the shaking boy while his other son searched around the deck. Reaching behind a bench, he grabbed what looked like a piece of ragged canvas, then brought it over and put it around the shivering kid.

Yes, they had watched it all. The binoculars were set back next to the deck chair. "Hey, do you think we should…" the man paused to take a deep drag from the smoke he was sharing. "We should…go help him?"

"No, not just yet." The balding cook leaned over and lifted the lid. "It looks like they are going to make it." He sniffed the aroma of the sizzling meat. "Chicken is done." He picked up tongs and started placing the pieces on the platter he held. "I'll pick this up quick, and then run over and see what we can do to help them. Don't want to ruin our fourth of July barbecue." He smiled at his friend sitting on the deck.

"Sure is good they had a life jacket on that kid, huh Rick?" The young man took a long drag, his straggly hair falling on his face as he spoke.

"Saved his life, that's for sure!" The cook set the plate down and walked back to the stern where his skiff was tied. Hopping over the rail and down the ladder, Rick jumped into the skiff. He gave a yank on the short, frayed cord, waking his little outboard engine from its dreams. Roaring to life, it sent the bow high into the air. He felt and heard the slap, slap, slap of water smacking under his feet as he pushed to full throttle. In seconds, he was at the boat of his

13

stranded neighbors.

"Need any help?" he called out cheerfully.

"I'd say that's just what we could use about now," replied the weary father of the shivering and soaked group. "I'm sure glad you came along."

"Is that little guy going to be all right?" yelled Rick. "It looked like he hit the side of the boat pretty hard."

"Yeah. He stopped crying as soon as he found out the sharks weren't going to eat him. He's hiding under the covers now." The man looked behind at a canvas lump near his feet. "But I have a family stranded on the beach waiting for me." He threw his hands down at his side, palms up in surrender. "My dinghy has sunk," he said woefully. "The boat we're floating on doesn't run, and it's at least a half-mile swim to the shore. Now we're in a worse mess than we were."

Rick was curious but refrained from asking any questions. "Well, let me take you over to my boat," he offered. "We'll get you warmed up. I can drop you off to recuperate while I get the rest of your group."

The grateful father nodded, "That would be great. You don't know how much I appreciate this."

The older boy jumped into the skiff. The man picked up the little boy and handed him down by the wrists to his big brother.

When he started to whimper, the brother comforted him, whispering, "Don't worry, Caleb. We aren't going very far. I promise the sharks won't get you. This boat won't sink."

The trembling child relaxed a little, but big tears continued to fall. Rick pointed to where he wanted the young man to sit. When he was satisfied that everyone's weight was safely balanced, he pointed the small craft through the choppy sea.

Water sprayed in their faces, and the child buried his head in his brother's arms, still whimpering.

Approaching the barnacled sides of the dark wooden relic, it would appear that this craft was even less seaworthy than the one they left. In truth, several bilge pumps were required to work around the clock keeping water out of it, but the visitors wouldn't need to be concerned with this information. The older boy nudged his brother out from under his wet jacket and shoved him toward the ladder. The scared kid looked back, wide-eyed at the threatening water with its white foamy arms splashing up and trying to grab him as he scrambled up the ladder. Strong arms covered him and gently guided to the deck.

Once on board, Rick led the family into the cabin. Several overstuffed leather chairs invited all comers to flop down. His friend had made a cozy fire, chasing the damp chill from the small space.

"Too bad about your dinghy," Rick said. "But you are lucky that kid is alive. This doesn't need to spoil your fourth of July holiday, though. I'll just ferry you guys back to shore when you are ready. We can probably get some divers here to search for your dinghy."

The boys sat down in a big, faded, brown chair and their dad began to rub his hands by the fire.

"You have to do it within two days, though, or you can kiss that engine goodbye," Rick said as he walked toward his small galley. "The salt water will eat it up."

Thanks again," said the man standing by the fire. "And by the way, my name is Glenn. These are my sons, Jason and Caleb." He glanced in the direction of the boys. Jason nodded politely at the introduction. Caleb looked at no one and said nothing.

Glenn continued, "Let me describe what I hope you find at the pier. I have two teenage daughters who should be sitting next to their sleeping bags at the end of the wharf. One of them will look totally depressed like she lost her best friend. You could pick her out of a crowd just by that. Her name is Holly. The other one is Jackie. She's rather unique, nothing like her sister. In fact, I would be surprised if you find her sitting by her bag like I told her. She is blond, thin, friendly, and probably off investigating something or other." The man chuckled as he thought about his girls. "Jackie is always in trouble, and Holly is usually mad about that or something else. My wife is at the parking lot with our other little boy, getting more gear. She was supposed to be the last pickup, so I don't think you will find her on the wharf yet. When you do find her, she will be carrying a mountain of stuff."

Rick stared straight ahead, listening to his guest and trying to imagine what he would do if he couldn't locate everyone. The bachelor of many years had virtually no experience with kids and no interest in getting any. He wondered how he was going to talk two young girls into getting in a boat with a perfect stranger and then leave to go out in the ocean. How big was this mountain of stuff, he worried, and how much weight was he volunteering to carry?

"Does Caleb want to watch cartoons?" he asked, looking to each face in turn. "I get three channels out here sometimes. We don't have cable service yet."

No one got the joke. They all looked at the little boy with raised eyebrows and hopeful smiles. Caleb promptly dove into his brother's stomach, hiding his face and clinging tightly. Rick wondered when the child would need to breathe.

Rick let out a sigh. "Well folks, make yourselves at home

while I go get the girls." He reached down and turned on the TV. The adventures of Batman blared into the room. Creaking, the fishing trawler gently rocked back and forth with the slow-moving breakers.

He stepped out of the cabin and looked out toward the palm tree, lined foothills just onshore with their row upon row of identical tiled roofs stacked like red and beige Lego blocks. Beautiful, and I am so lucky to be here, he thought. His little piece of real estate in the sea was set up in such a way that the wave action was considerably less than what most boats suffered in the moorings. A place of legal homelessness existed in Free Harbor for those who didn't mind parking themselves just off the coast, and it was possible to live in the glorious paradise of the rich. The poor who managed to stay had to sacrifice all of their earnings just to garner a little spot in the beautiful city of year-round, perfect weather.

Many boat owners couldn't live on their boats, but Rick could. The moorings were free but dangerous. He looked around as he stepped into his skiff. Boats of all sizes and shapes bobbed like corks around the perimeter of Stearns Wharf pier. After every storm, moorings would break and tiny, floating, weekend retreats would become more driftwood littering the beaches, beached whales rotting upon the white sands all because their owner failed to bring them into the harbor when the need arose. With much effort, this rugged man of the sea had managed to keep his afloat, bringing it in at the first sign of strong winds or waves. He was proud he had hung onto his little chunk of floating paradise for so many years.

Glenn stepped out onto the deck and waved after him. "Thanks again, buddy," he hollered, watching the man speed off toward the harbor.

As Rick passed the Tabitha, he wondered how the family the man described would squeeze into that small cabin. A seagull perched on the railing, a squatter in the absence of the owners.

"Where are they all planning to fit?" Rick called out to it and then laughed, shaking his head.

Waves splashed over the bow of his skiff as he raced the quarter mile to the pier. Brown and white pelicans swooped and dove in front of him. At the end of the wharf, Rick saw an attractive young girl around twelve or thirteen leaning against a huge, wooden log used for seating. Sitting on a sleeping bag, she was hugging a pillow and chewing on a long, blond braid. Her toes were pushed underneath a blue, gym bag, and lost in her thoughts she never noticed Rick's approach. Two large pelicans stood as motionless sentries by her side, but the sad eyes stared straight ahead, unaware.

"Hey, kid!" he called out. "I'm here to give you a ride. Your daddy's boat had a little accident."

Big, beautiful, green eyes opened wide as they turned in slow motion to focus upon the stranger. Her face displayed the struggle of dealing with this interruption.

"You're Holly, aren't you?" His tone was cheerful.

Those eyes glared, piercing him with a hard stare. "What do you mean...an accident?" Each word enunciated as she focused intently on this middle-aged man before her in ragged, tan t-shirt and hiking shorts.

"Uh...Uh," Rick stammered under the glare coming from this young woman—creature. Yeah, I wouldn't trust me either, he thought. Smart girl. He spoke again, choosing the words carefully.

"Your dad's dinghy sunk. They were trying to board the Tabitha. Everyone is okay, but the little boat is gone. I have a boat and it's moored next to your family's. Your dad sent me to pick you up."

Rick paused and watched her process these new developments. She began to take on more of the appearance of a trusting child.

"Would that be okay?" Rick asked gently. He took off his sunglasses and waited. Another large, brown pelican flapped behind Holly, landing beside the log. The girl remained unaware. She continued to stare intently at this strange man whom she had never seen before and who was bringing very disturbing news.

Rick continued, "Is your sister here?"

Still wary, Holly answered, "Yeah, she's right over there. I'll get her." She turned and looked at a skinny, taller girl in a short, white jumpsuit standing near the fish market.

"Jackie!" she yelled. Again she yelled, but louder and more insistent this time. "Jackie, get over here!"

Jackie, distracted by birds or fishermen or both, pretended not to hear.

Holly gathered her possessions together and looked back at her sister. "I know you can hear me," she shouted. "Dad said we have to ride with him." She turned back to acknowledge Rick with a pointed finger.

Alighting from her spot on the log, Holly handed her things down to the hefty man standing on the ladder. Rick descended with bags balanced and bobbing off his arms and back. Holly glanced down at the balding head and tattered shorts of the stranger and wondered what had happened in the short time her Dad had said, "Wait here. I'll be back in five minutes."

She turned around to begin her descent and yelled one more time. "Hurry up, Jackie! Quit wasting time! Let's go!"

This time her sister decided to respond and danced along the rail as she made her way to the ladder. She was ecstatic, totally inebriated with joy and life. Trusting as a friendly puppy, the young girl jumped in the boat with no thought to question the situation and obediently sat where Rick pointed.

"Hi, I'm Jackie," she said, tossing her head like a young filly shaking its mane. "Is this your boat? Where are we going? Why are we doing this again?" she peppered Rick, barely pausing to catch a breath and not caring to hear any answers. The girl was like the sunshine dancing and jumping off the waves. She reached down and splashed in the water with a cupped hand.

"We are going to where Dad is. The little boat sunk," Holly growled at her. "This guy picked them up or something."

"Oh," said Jackie. "Well, that was good." She paused, then said, "Not good about the boat sinking, I mean, but good you picked them up." She glanced over at Rick, then closed her eyes and turned her face into the spray as the boat sped out from the wharf and away from the channel.

"Wow! This is really fast! I love your boat! This is cool!" Jackie chattered over the roar of the noisy outboard.

Disaster would not slow this one down, Rick thought. Here was a kid seriously intent on enjoying every minute. He mused at the two girls' differences as he raced them back to their family. At the boat, he cut the engine, slowly pulling the skiff to his ladder. He grabbed each girl's hand to steady them as they stepped up. A ladder would have been helpful for the Tabitha.

"Go on inside the cabin, girls, and watch TV if you want," Rick offered. Firing up the motor, he hollered, "I'm going back to get your mom, now." In an instant, the boat turned and sped off.

Clutching her bags, Holly surveyed the deck of the old fishing relic. Not impressed, she viewed it with an air of disdain.

The other sister clapped her hands and shouted, "TV way out here? Can you believe it?" She leaped toward the cabin door in a hurry to verify this amazing development.

"Oh, my!" she yelled back at her sister. "It's working and everything. Come and see."

Jackie entered the cabin, and her eyes slowly adjusted to the darkened room. "Oh, hi Jason. Hey, everybody's here. Why is everybody here?"

Jason just shook his head. "Never mind, Jackie. Just never mind. We'll be going back to our boat soon."

In a few minutes, Rick arrived with a dazed and bewildered lady. Surrounded by many black plastic bags, she was holding onto a skinny, tow-headed kid who kept looking around and poking into every new thing. At the moment, the outboard had his full attention. From the deck, everyone assembled to greet this new arrival with a piece of the information.

"What do you mean he almost drowned?" The black bag she had been handing to her husband dropped. "What are you saying?" She glared at him. Moments passed as the shocked lady processed the news. Speech returned.

"He hit the what? He fell into the water? What are you saying?" Shaking her head in disbelief, she scrambled up the ladder and now stood before them.

"You mean to tell me he could have been carried out to sea by the current?" She looked at them incredulously, staring at each of them in turn as though one of them might tell her that none of this was true, none of this had ever happened. Moments passed. No one said a word.

"Well, I guess I should be getting you folks back to your boat," interrupted Rick. He was feeling very uncomfortable at this little family display of mother meltdown. Sad faces looked toward him and heads began to nod silently.

Rick graciously ferried the castaways to the Tabitha, then helped them navigate the difficulty of boarding without a ladder. He turned and waved a final gesture. The family sat staring as he sped away, each one in silent contemplation regarding their precarious state. They were adrift without even a blow-up swim ring to paddle ashore. They were now at the mercy of the whims of the next-door neighbor whom they had just met. He only lived as far away as the next set of waves, but so far as they could tell they hadn't managed to make a favorable impression.

Moving into action, Susan grabbed a plastic bag beside her. "Anyone want a sandwich? I brought plenty. Girls?" Susan pleaded while holding out the bag to them. "Anyone?"

Jason leaned over and grabbed the bag, then started wolfing down sandwiches. Both girls shook their heads no and began pulling out sleeping bags from the black trash bags. They were claiming their territory and setting up housekeeping, dragging their beds-for-the-night out onto the bow. Their mother took note of the fact there was no deck railing, and it was open to the sea.

"No, girls. That doesn't look at all safe. Bring those back here," she called after them.

Both girls groaned, reluctantly dragging the bags back to the safer deck. Caleb was lying at his brother's feet, not moving. His eyes were shut tight but he was not asleep. Out over the horizon, brilliant explosions of light began to appear in the sky.

"Look, kids!" their father shouted. "Fireworks! You can see fireworks!"

"Cabey, Look!" His mother gave his shoulder a gentle shake. Look at the pretty lights, honey. It's fourth of July."

Caleb whimpered and squeezed his eyes shut. He pulled himself tighter into a little ball, trying to cover more of his head with one arm.

"Caleb, you're missing the fireworks. This is when we celebrate our freedom."

The child, unaware of freedom and not interested in fireworks, only wanted to sleep. Perhaps to escape the memory of the previous few hours, his mother thought. She gave up and went over to her husband who was leaning against the rail. Arm-in arm they stood, watching the colors reflect on the water.

"Praise the Lord," she whispered. "It's beautiful over the water. It reminds me of the part in the song "rockets red glare, the bombs bursting in air." How ironic that on our first day of having to leave our home it would be Independence Day?"

Glenn looked at his wife. "Yes, I was just thinking the same thing. It's all about freedom."

God's loyal love couldn't have run out, his merciful love couldn't have dried up. They're created new every morning. They're created new every morning. How great your faithfulness! I'm sticking with God (I say it over and over). He's all I've got left.

Lamentations 3:22-24 "The Message"

Awakening

Homeless and marooned on a chunk of floating, dead wood, the little group of slumbering refugees began to rouse as the brilliant sun burst through the horizon. The piercing rays splashed the faces of the sleeping couple lying just underneath the hatch cover that had been thrown back the previous night. Children buried under canvas were safe from discovery awhile longer, as was the young toddler cuddled in as close as he could melt next to his parents. He was hiding under the blankets to escape the damp, sea air.

Plopped into the center of the roomy V-berth was a large, white futon surrounded by faded, paisley cushions the couple managed to scrounge from previous household belongings. Maybe pillows didn't completely cover the bare wood of the berth, but they provided some insulation and extended the bed. Silently looking around for the first time, Susan rocked with the gentle slap, slap, slap of the waves against the bow. She watched light dance off the bare wood in the stripped down interior, her eyes focusing on the few timbers covered with remaining staples where old upholstery had been ripped. Its naked primitiveness was a stark reality against the glory of the new day. She laid there waiting for some time, hoping to hear the sound of the neighbor's skiff racing toward them for the promised ride into harbor. She might have dozed off with no way to know for how long. Gulls called down, awakening her. She heard their screeching and squawking, and looked up to see them playing tag and chasing each other under a scattering of clouds. The open hatch let the breeze cool the mid-summer air while stirring around the ocean smells like a salt-water stew in a large old pot. Susan watched her husband pull the covers away from their little boy's head, giving him fresh air. He snuggled in closer to his father's side.

"I wish I had gone camping at least some time in my life," she whispered to her groggy husband.

"Yeah. Me too," he said.

They both lie listening to the sounds of something stirring on deck. "Kids are getting up," said Susan.

Glenn glanced at his wife. "Rick said he was coming over early, but I don't think his early will get me to work on time."

Trying not to think of the call they'd have to make to the boss, the couple lay basking under the false cheerfulness of the bright morning flooding their new home. Nearby, the high whine of an outboard broke the silence.

"Praise the Lord!" Glenn said. "It's Rick, finally. Let's get the crew in gear."

Susan sat up, and a wave of nausea threw her back on the mattress. Trying again, she reached over and grabbed the hand rails, pulling herself up to the deck above. Peeking under an old orange tarp, she cheerfully announced, "Come alive, you guys! We're going. Time to get up now."

Another wave of seasickness sent her scrambling back to the futon. She looked over at her husband dressing in the cabin, taking notice he didn't seem to be having any trouble.

"Mom, I'm sick. When does this go away?" moaned Jackie, peering in through the doorway at her mother who was attempting once again to stand on her feet.

"I can't take this being out here. I'm sick too," cried Holly. "When can we get off this boat?" She laid on the deck whimpering, no longer trying to get up.

Susan stumbled out in the fresh air. "Look at the land. It helps a lot," she said. "This is my best trick, though. Just tilt your head sideways as though you were lying down. I don't know why it works, but it does."

"Oh Mom, it's just your imagination," complained Holly, once more trying to sit up. She grabbed a small, black purse and beach sandals for the ride back. "Nothing is going to make this go away except to get back on land. I can't take this. I really can't. We don't even have a bathroom. I can't believe you are making us come out here. I don't see how you could do this to us." Holly's face clearly showed her despair.

She flung up her arms, exasperated. "This thing could even sink! You don't know if it's going down in the night while we are sleeping."

At the sound of his sister's cry, Kelly popped up like a little spring from his perch on the hard deck, blond hair sticking up in every direction. "I don't know what is the matter with you girls. There's nothing wrong with me," he said, taking particular delight at the opportunity to goad his sisters in their suffering. "Mom, why do we have to wear these life jackets anyway when we are sleeping? They are not exactly comfortable, you know."

Susan's heart broke hearing her daughter's cries. She struggled to find answers, but no words would come. If only she could relieve their suffering, but Susan was completely helpless, and waves of desperation crashed over engulfing the mother's heart. Compounding the misery was the constant nausea. Truth was, there was a possibility that she might have to watch her children drown before her eyes, but at the moment the ocean consuming them now was one of fear. In this life or death situation, wrong attitudes could finish them off quicker than the threat of the surrounding waters smacking against the sides of their boat.

"Holly, in the future if we start to sink, wake me up!" Her voice was sharp. "I'll be below you in the cabin, okay? You'll probably survive, although we may not. I can just picture it." Her voice had begun to rise, increasing to a shout to be heard over the sound of Rick's approaching motor. In moments he would be here, Susan thought, watching him circle in his approach to pull alongside.

"You kids above deck will be floating away onto shore while we will be going down, glug, glug, glug. Be sure and tell them your mom drowned at sea because she didn't want to break the law and risk losing all of you." Hot tears spilled over. "Tell them she dragged you out into the ocean and risked your life because," Susan's voice cracked, "...it was the only way to be homeless and still obey the law."

Holly stared steadily at her mother, shaking her head, not accepting any of it.

Susan searched her daughter's face looking for a sign of any connection. "Tell them things didn't go the way she planned either, that your mom was afraid too. Oh yeah, and be sure to tell them your mom felt helpless...often.

Holly folded her arms across her chest and turned away. The words had only pushed her further from her mother. It wasn't working.

"One more thing, Holly. Don't forget I will always believe the Lord will provide for us no matter how desperate the accommodations." In a more soothing tone, she said, "Try to think of this as a large, floating cradle gently rocking you to sleep at night."

"Oh yeah, sure, Mom. Well, I don't see why we can't get in a house like normal people," she spit out the hot, angry words. "You just want to live like hippies for some strange reason I don't know. This boat doesn't even have the things other boats have, no running water, no lights, shower, sink, stove, fridge, table, chair, nothing!" Holly punctuated the last word with a rising voice, dripping with anger. "And what's worse, the engine doesn't run. You have to have it towed out here to tie it up!"

Each word was heard and felt as an arrow tipped with poison to her mother's soul. Holly turned her head at the sound of Rick cutting his engine, and ceased from the tirade as she watched him tie up.

"It floats," her mom retorted. "And right now that is all it needs to do. We have a porta-potty for emergencies and bottled water if you get thirsty. You are probably going to be fine in spite of all this, but the good news is we are getting you back on land now." Her mother handed her a life jacket. "You can be first trip back."

Jackie had been quiet, sitting and hugging her stomach while listening to the unfolding drama. She brightened up at the sound of the other boat. "Hi! Good morning!" she hollered out to Rick.

"First crew ready to go," Susan called out to Rick with false cheerfulness, wiping her eyes with an arm and clearing her throat to recover her voice. She handed him bags of leftover sandwiches from the night before and a sack of laundry and trash.

"All right! Who is going on the first? We are gonna have to take a couple trips," Rick announced." He quickly stowed the packages under the seats.

Holly jumped over the rail and hopped down. "I am," she said as Rick steadied and guided her to where he wanted.

"You go with the boys, Suzi," Glenn said as he lowered the six-year-old into the skiff. I will come next trip with Jackie and Jason."

"All right you guys. Here we come!" Susan shouted as she grabbed up a chubby little wrist belonging to the toddler who'd been clinging to her leg. She passed Caleb into the boat. He started to cry again until she sat beside him, grabbing and holding him tight.

"We are not going to sink, Cabey. Don't worry." She tried to comfort him as the engines were revved and turned to face the sea heading toward the channel.

Yeah, don't worry, Susan worried. Oh, if only they had been given just a few more hours to leave their house, and if only Glenn hadn't been so exhausted trying to accommodate the wishes of another. Maybe he wouldn't have made such a simple but near-fatal mistake. Susan's thoughts went back to the previous day's events when she had seen him so tired he couldn't walk straight after returning from the all day loading of possessions into the storage room. He had complained to her then of how he had been caught in long lines of traffic at the beach and begged the cop for a way around. The cop had told him he picked the wrong day to move. He hated that it caused him to lose precious daylight hours for everything he still had to do.

She had been exhausted from cleaning and moving out, and had begged to wait until morning to leave. There is nothing the landlord can do she said, but Glenn remained determined to comply with the demand. Her husband would never stand up to someone else and demand that his own needs should come first. He lived his life trying to do what others expected and that's what he would always do. And then, as though remembering who it was she was upset with, Susan softened. This was what made her husband special and one of the things that she loved so much about him.

"So what now, Lord?" Susan muttered under her breath, although no one except the Lord would be able to hear her above the sound of the motor. "What is going to happen to us? How are you going to get us out of this?"

The brisk pace of the little skiff racing through the channel was exhilarating, and Caleb perked up and seemed to enjoy the ride as much as his mother. The spray hitting their faces was cooling and exciting, and Susan's nausea was subsiding allowing her to enjoy all of the approaching harbor sights and sounds. This would be her second boat ride ever, not counting previous Disneyland adventures. The taste of the wind splashing across her face salted the air, and the massive pier pilings of Stearns Wharf threatened to swallow the small skiff as they skirted the edge. Nearby, seagulls chased and squawked at a fishing boat laboring to drag home its heavy load. Yachts slowly paraded in and out of the harbor channel waving friendly greetings as they passed. Susan looked toward the hills and saw windows from all the houses in the city shining back at her like diamonds, their reflection caught from the sun, twinkling and sparkling as land jewels decorating the water's edge. She took in the sights all around her, the first day of a new life.

Yesterday's shock mixed with fear and this morning's sorrow with her children had tried to creep in to spoil this new day, but none of it had the power to prevent what was happening at the moment. Maybe it had been the ship's whistle sound or the happy squawks from the gulls being fed on the docks by tourists, or the harbor seal suddenly rearing its head from close range and barking a friendly warning. It could be that this new memory of absolute stillness and peaceful escape from the world while being gently rocked to sleep throughout the night was responsible. Maybe it was the beautiful lights last night along the shore gently reminding her that civilization was just a short swim away. Whatever the cause, Susan could not wait to return to this watery world. She discovered that she was in love with being at sea.

"So don't worry about tomorrow, for tomorrow will bring its own worries. Today's trouble is enough for today.

Matthew 6:34 New Living Translation

Wing and a Prayer

Once they were all back on shore, Rick announced he was heading for the showers.

"Mom, we need the card so we can get showers too," Holly begged.

"Here you go." Her mom handed it over. "Don't lose it. We have to pay to have it replaced." She waved them off and then returned to the more important business of getting her husband to work.

Glenn spoke what she had been worrying. "Hope it starts this morning."

They walked the short distance to where their golden, vintage "classic" now sat alone in the big, empty, parking lot. A citation on the windshield was their friendly greeting.

"What is this for?" Glenn snapped it off angrily. He looked up after reading it, and marched over to a nearby parking sign. He hadn't noticed the warning that parking was prohibited from 3:00 AM to 5:00 AM. Turning the ticket over, he looked at the back. "Twenty-two dollars," he said sadly, shaking his head. "That would have bought a sleeping bag for Kelly or Jason."

"Let's just get you to your job and don't worry about it now," Susan said. She had a huge chunk of problems of her own to solve and needed to get started. Her plans included a third trip back to the DMV to finish getting the registration for an old, converted, school bus they had in storage. She hoped the requested two hundred and fifteen dollars would satisfy the nice lady, and she could finally walk away with the precious, little, red sticker.

"Try it again, Glenn," encouraged his wife, but the battery refused even a click. This car was taking no one anywhere on this morning. Put this on the list of things to deal with later, Susan thought, as they crossed the street where they had parked their aging but more reliable Corvair.

"Just do your job and don't worry about the problems," Susan tried to reassure.

"Don't exactly have a choice right now, do I?" Glenn rode the few miles in silence.

They had watched their family slowly getting squeezed for a long time. Forced from most options, Glenn hadn't been able to protect them from any of it. It had been a struggle for many years just to keep food on the table, but with both of them working they had been able to keep off public assistance. Susan thought back to the years of living in trailers and staying with friends. There had been a couple of disasters. Once when they had been forced into tents, it flooded. The other time was when their travel trailer jackknifed, and only Glenn's stubborn determination to obey the law had saved the children's lives. They had been asleep in the back and Susan didn't want to wake them for the short, four-mile journey, but he'd said it wasn't legal. She'd argued they weren't living in an old "I Love Lucy" rerun and nothing should go wrong, but he'd insisted, and they'd been brought into the truck. The hitch they had installed that day failed going down the first hill, and their travel trailer was totaled. The Highway Patrol said the children would have been killed, and Susan was forever grateful Glenn had not listened to her.

Then there was the continual struggle with vehicles breaking down while being forced to move from campground to campground just to keep within the law. It had been a hard life for the children.

"See you later, honey." He kissed her goodbye and trudged, shoulders slumped, up the short hill to his job.

She thought back over the past year spent living in luxury accommodations when she had landed a job as a caretaker for a mentally disabled man. It had been more of a project than a job. Phil had lived his entire life in institutions until his younger brother found a way to change that. For many years this brother had wanted to set him free, and after meeting Susan he believed she could help him pull it off. He'd invited the whole family into his eight-bedroom home in Mission Canyon. Springing Phil from an institutionalized life sentence was a noble endeavor in itself, but even heavily medicated the schizophrenic, child-like man had presented many problems that kept everyone stressed.

She thought back to the many times when her husband had walked into the room and found Phil choking her ever so gently and whispering, "Phil don't like dogs, Phil don't like dogs." With the sweat dripping off his face, white-lipped and shaking, Phil would then run and jump on the furniture or run frantically around the yard, only returning to grab her neck once again and whisper, "Phil don't like dogs."

She'd handled the crazy behaviors well enough, usually by pushing his hands away and handing him another tablet from the bottle she kept with her. The kids had learned to get Phil newspapers to tear up or else quickly sidestep him whenever they saw him coming. Glenn never could relax. There was always the tension of not knowing for whom he might have to call 911.

It took a few months, but the miracle had occurred. New

routines were established, and Phil became a rather contented fellow. It was even possible for Susan to take him out in public and then to church with her. Phil loved church. The couple felt successful in dealing with the many challenges they faced in their unique situation, but then came the signs that the doors were closing, and they both knew it was time to begin their search again in the ongoing game of survival.

The idea of living at sea was first introduced when Glenn found an old wooden boat that someone was discarding. He was buzzing with excitement as he shared the possibility. They had been struggling with the temptation to leave Santa Barbara, but they both knew that would not be wise. He would never find a job as good as the one he had. When Jason overheard them talking, he informed his parents that if they decided to leave he would not be going with them. Glenn couldn't blame him. Jason and his mom had a typesetting business that was in its infancy, and until it generated more income they needed to discover some creative but legal way to hold their fragile little group together. They all agreed the boat might provide the legal loophole that would help them get established. They could stay in the harbor about half of the time, and the rest of the month their boat would provide a floating hotel.

It had been easy enough to find a mechanic. It only took a couple of weeks to have the engine rebuilt, but then the problems with the transmission were discovered. Another month, another check, Glenn had said, and he was confident he could pull it off. It had been a plan—shaky, but a plan.

Phil's brother had waited until Glenn came into the kitchen to grab his coffee one fateful morning. Then as Susan was making breakfast, he handed her a Three Day Notice to Vacate. The couple stood in shock and disbelief listening silently to the polite lecture.

"Can't you give us just a little bit of time, even a couple more weeks?"

But no, he wouldn't. In just another month, Glenn agonized, the boat would have been viable, but their housing situation had come to a surprising and abrupt end, and neither it nor they were ready.

Standing before the huge, carved doors of the Presbyterian Church, Glenn just stopped. He seemed to be lost in his thoughts, momentarily stuck. Susan watched him, thinking back to when he first got the job as janitor for the big church on the hill. It was the best he had ever had, and he had felt honored to be able to serve the Lord in such a humble capacity. His heart was thankful every day he went to work, and he always had something good to say about the job. This would be a decent salary in most areas he had said, and Glenn's employment possibilities were limited.

A few years back some thugs had piped him in the head one night while he'd been standing on the Ventura pier. The brain damage had been severe, and he was left with recurring and debilitating headaches, but he let go of a disability stipend to work at doing whatever he could find. He would do anything for Suzi and the kids. She was thankful and appreciated everything about him, and she hated what was happening to him now. She watched him stand staring at the door for a few moments. Then without looking back, he went inside.

Susan drove down Anacapa to the DMV, and an hour later while waiting for her turn Susan shut her eyes and pictured this new home she was so desperate to get licensed. The stack of papers she held in her hands stated it was a converted school bus. Converted was a misnomer she thought, but they had managed to get a roof on, and the skylights were installed—six of them in fact, blasting the whole interior with enough light to chase away the depressing emptiness. The original roof had been cut off, and a large dowel and peg wooden-framed cabin built on top allowing for a roomy, nine feet of interior height. Glenn had covered the wood framing with redwood cedar paneling, inside and out. A few loft areas had been hung from the rafters allowing treehouse-style bedrooms for the kids, and some rustic wood and rope knotted ladders had been crafted to allow the kids to get into them.

Susan didn't like to think about the remaining barren walls below the upper cabin with official emergency door insignia, some graffiti, and the chipped, aqua paint of more than twenty years still hanging onto the double-walled steel. There also wasn't much in the way of furnishings, but the bus almost had a galley. A heavy, press-board cabinet with a walnut-stained top stood next to a three-piece bar unit that had been given to the scavengers. This dumpster-dive piece of furniture with the sliding, thick, wooden doors would be their only cabinet space. The thing most lacking in their galley was a working stove. Without 220V, the two electric burners were not going to help, and the refrigerator wouldn't be useful either except as a tiny cabinet. The twelve-inch sink could hold water, but drained to nothing except a hole in the floor. This roughly drilled orifice led directly outside.

She remembered the day she had helped build a small room near the rear. They had hopes of one day turning it into a shower. She had glued the tiny pink tiles onto the floor herself, and into this had installed another drain leading to nowhere. Might as well not worry, thought Susan. No plumbing, no faucets, no incoming water lines, no sinks, no holding tanks, no hot water tanks...so no problems at all with any of it.

"Number eleven," a lady in a gray and white-vested suit announced.

Susan looked down at her number. Seventeen. Next to her the boys were absolute angels, sitting on the chair and swinging their legs back and forth while watching the lines of people pass by.

Going back to her daydreams, she began to worry about their little porta-potty with the missing cap. It's going to smell throughout the whole bus she thought, but at least we will have some privacy. Maybe I can tie a plastic bag around it. She remembered when they had ceremoniously placed the plastic throne in the shower stall, thinking the little room should have a purpose until the day came when it could be finished. Old, louvered, closet doors found in an abandoned garage had transformed nicely into a door. Susan had tacked mirrors up against the outside wall of their "bathroom", and Caleb's short bunk bed had been built across the top of it forming the ceiling.

Two hundred and forty square feet of internal space for seven people she mentally calculated. She had been upset with her husband when he first wanted to buy the huge, naked monstrosity. She hadn't wanted to pay storage for it either. He had told her he never wanted them to be homeless again. He'd talked her into it by telling her if they got it they would always have a home. He'd been right. She was glad now.

"We are modern day Swiss Family Robinson," she said to the boys. Their blank stares reminded her they were too young to have heard that story.

Yes, conversion had a long way to go Susan thought, but the bus was the backup plan, and that was just what the family needed now. Backup.

"Number seventeen."

I'm not trying to get my way in the world's way. I'm trying to get your way, your Word's way. I'm staying on your trail; I'm putting one foot in front of the other. I'm not giving up. I call to you, God, because I'm sure of an answer. So—answer! Bend your ear! Listen sharp! Paint grace-graffiti on the fences; take in your frightened children who are running from the neighborhood bullies straight to you. Keep your eye on me; hide me under your cool wing feathers.

Psalm 17:4-8 –The Message Translation

The Breaking

During the panic of the move and in their urgency the couple had made the decision to store their possessions in Glenn's office at his place of work. No one ever went into it, and it was far removed from other offices and classrooms. At the time, they didn't realize what a monstrous mess it would all become.

Glenn unlocked the door for his wife to look for things she needed, then returned to his vacuuming. The boys searched with their eyes finding everything they were sure they couldn't live without. Standing in the middle of the room, Susan stared at the conglomeration of hurriedly packed boxes all crazily stacked and stuffed in a haphazard fashion. She saw girl's shirts mixed with Christmas ornaments, one shoe tangled with a lamp chord, and in another box the matching shoe mixed with Lego blocks. There were dishes in a box with cleaning supplies, and canned food with books. She faced the fact that everything she owned was suddenly lost. They needed so many things, if only they could be found.

"Why can't singing beh-wa come wiff us now, Mommy? Why do he haff to stay in da box?" Caleb tugged on his mother's hand.

What do I say to a three-year-old when I know I have to fill my arms with coats, sweaters, can openers, and extra silverware, Susan agonized? She wondered how important singing bear was in times like these.

The boys spied many of their treasures, wanting to grab

them all.

"Dair is Pow-eh Wan-geh, Kellwie! Git em." Caleb shouted and pointed at the floor.

Kelly dropped to his knees in a flash. Power Ranger was snatched from where it had fallen and quickly stuffed inside a jean pocket.

Susan groaned. This was too hard. She reached over and grabbed the bear, handing it to the toddler and swiped at his tears with her shirt-sleeve.

"Tonka stays in the box, okay, Kelly?" She had to draw the line somewhere.

Kelly nodded, ever the big brother and trying to act wise beyond his years. She handed him some coats that had been stuffed in a black, plastic bag, and he bravely threw it behind his back looking like a little Santa Claus carrying his burden. He looked at his mother expectantly, waiting for her to go. She stared at the sweet, trusting face and then reached over impulsively, grabbed the toy truck, and put it in his other hand. He smiled and silently trotted behind her to the car.

The next morning proved to be another episode of coming in late. Rick had been gracious with ferrying them back and forth, but his schedule was quite a bit different than theirs. The bus after receiving the magic, paper sticker on its license plate became the daytime residence of the Dunns. All heads had turned at the magnificence of the twelve-and-a-half foot tall cabin driving down Cabrillo Blvd for the first time. Traffic slowed then stopped while people gawked, watching it turn into the harbor lot. It was beautiful to behold, scary coming down the road, but beautiful. It now occupied two parking spaces daily which was legal, and it was legal for the family to remain inside. It was also legal for the bus to remain overnight in the harbor lot, but the people could not. In this town it was not legal for the homeless to sleep. They would need to be in the water in order to sleep without breaking the law.

Susan looked over at the inflatable, three-man raft where it had been neatly folded and placed on a high shelf. Their friend, Patrick, had brought it by and loaned it to them the day after the dinghy sunk. "Glenn, I think it will work," she said pointing to it.

Glenn scrambling to get changed for work grabbed a chocolate doughnut lying on a napkin. "Suzi, everyone I talk to thinks we are crazy, that I don't care about you guys. Did you know that? And I feel like this is all my fault."

"But I see people going out in them every day. We could just get a little motor. I know the raft will work for us." She tried to put her arms around him, tried to find some way to put back together her poor, broken husband, but he just stared blankly.

"The boat is almost fixed, and we're only talking money and a little time," she began again, "...and we'll be back on track."

"No!" He pulled away abruptly. "We're talking risking the life of my family in a big inner tube that could just pop!" He was yelling at her now. "And I'm not gonna do it!"

He jumped down out of the bus and walked away. The conversation was over.

As he stepped away, Susan watched an officer of the Harbor Patrol walk up to him.

"Hi, I'm Officer Mike..."

She pushed the doors open a little bit so she could hear better what was being said. Her husband carefully explained their whole sad story. The cop seemed friendly and understanding enough. He pointed to a place on the lot where the boat trailers were and said he would talk to his supervisor to see if they could be allowed to park there. She heard him say it might facilitate easing them into the harbor community in general.

"One day they might propose an ordinance to get rid of you," he laughed as he walked away. "Continuing to take showers in the Marina could cause problems for me in the future, but for now we'll see what happens. Keep me informed."

Glenn left visibly relaxed and cheered. Sharing the burden with local law enforcement had brought such a relief. Cops had always been Susan's heroes, and she had turned to them for help many times in her life. Now she could quit worrying and concentrate on getting to work. Maybe later she might even figure out how to operate the Coleman gas stove Rick had so kindly offered to them.

Holly interrupted her mother's thoughts. "Can we go to Jennifer and Adolph's today? They want to take us surfing, and then after that we will have youth group." She stood near the door holding a small duffel slung over her shoulder. Her sister was stuffing a bathing suit into her backpack.

Jackie smiled and nodded her head up and down like a little puppet. "Please, Mom. They said we're no trouble at all. Oh, please let us go. We get so sick, and it doesn't go away."

Holly looked steadily into her mother's eyes. "Adolph said we could stay with them whenever you go out on the boat. We'll be fine."

In just the few days the family had begun catching rides out to free harbor the girls managed to invent their own survival plan. The youth ministers at a local church were trusted family friends of the Dunns who loved to collect kids and do things with them. They liked to surf a lot, and the girls went to everything their outreach offered.

"They said they feel sorry for you guys too, and they just want to help. Can we go?" Holly begged.

Her mother caught her breath at those gorgeous, green eyes. She tried to remember back a year or so when the girls were going away to their first summer camp. They had seemed so small. Hadn't this happened too fast? Hadn't they just sold the Barbie Dolls at the last yard sale? She noticed that her daughter's long, blond hair had been neatly brushed and tied back into a ponytail, and she was once again wearing her favorite jeans with rips and tears. Holly had tied a faded, blue hoody around her waist in case the t-shirt would not be warm enough. Jackie only wanted shorts and tank tops, and would never wear anything that could be called a jacket. A quick swipe through her hair with a brush and she was ready to go. They were growing up so fast, bold and confident. Her girls were precious, and a gnawing feeling of uneasiness was growing in the pit of her stomach. She couldn't choose. She just couldn't, but a decision had to be made, and she fought for the courage to make it.

"Okay," she said finally. "But you can't keep going there. You live with us. Do you understand? We are your family."

"Thanks, Mom," they both yelled, turning and running with their packs bouncing on their backs. They raced toward the boardwalk to catch the free shuttle. Susan stood watching them through the bus window unaware she was still waving after they were out of sight.

One more night the girls would be safe from the trip out to the boat. One more night. Susan began to hate the necessity which sent the rest of them out to sea. One more night the feeling of impending disaster would continue to grow. They were being divided.

They push the needy off the road; all the poor of the land are forced to hide.

Job 24:4 New King James Version

Unraveling

"Beans again tonight?" The weary voice asked somewhat sarcastically.

The street light illuminated the darkened bus through the skylights, but all movement inside occurred in deep shadows. Another long day at work coming home to the dark; another night scurrying around to get ready to go out to dinner. With no water system it was not possible to clean up or prepare meals, and without a kitchen there could be no cooking. There wasn't time for trips to the store either. Up at seven and bed past eleven, and that would be on a good night. Susan could not care for her family in any of the ways she knew, but one thing remained unchanged. They could still go to work.

"I'm gonna barf if I have to eat any more hot dogs," Holly complained.

"At least you're eating now," her older brother scolded.

It was their new habit to attend the nightly service at the local Rescue Mission. If they hurried they were able to get in before the doors locked at seven, and an hour later after a few favorite songs and another salvation message they would walk away with plates of beans, hot dogs, buckets of cottage cheese, and bags of doughnuts. The three teens refused to go. Scores of ragged, smelly men did not appeal to them, and the only other families in attendance were usually those involved with the ministry of the nightly, church service. Susan felt out-of-place too, never having time to change out of her dress and heels, and Caleb never got to eat as it was virtually impossible to keep him awake through the lengthy sermon.

Pulling up to the curb on this evening, they had been interrupted by a tall, young man walking toward them as they prepared to enter.

"Hello. My name is Alan, and I've been wanting to meet you. I'm so impressed with your bus and your family. I think it's amazing what you have done, and you have a beautiful family! I've been truly envious of everything I've heard. Excuse me for being so bold, but I had to meet you. I work for the city, and I'm also in the program here. I see your boat whenever it comes into the harbor." He reached to shake hands with Glenn and nodded toward Susan and the kids.

"Hello," Glenn said cheerfully. "Pleased to meet you, Alan. Glad to hear positive encouragement anytime."

"Oh yes! You have a wonderful family," he gushed. "I am so pleased to finally meet you. If there is anything I can ever do to help just let me know. Enjoy your evening." He turned and walked quickly back toward the mission.

Alan would become a daily visitor, cheering everyone whenever he showed up. This night, however, would be a repeat of the ongoing challenge of feeding all the members of the family.

"I can't wake him up, no matter what I try," she implored the director for help, trying not to cry. At that moment two hundred men had been singing "I've Got a Mansion Just Over the Hilltop" so loud that the rafters were shaking, but he had remained slumped over his bear.

"Caleb, honey. You have to eat—you never get to eat." When Caleb was out for the night, it didn't matter what his mother tried. He would never respond. Another night would pass, piling up the guilt she was carrying.

The kind staff had tried bending the rules by letting her walk around with him in the waiting room, hoping it would keep him awake, but he would flop down on the overstuffed sofa and pass out. The cooks fell in love with the sleepy toddler padding around in his footed pajamas and clinging to singing bear. They had each taken turns walking him around the building to see the fish tank or meet the cook or try any idea they could think of to keep the kid awake. But bedtime was bedtime for this little guy, and nothing was changing that.

On one particular evening the cook announced to the tired mother, "We have a new rule. You can leave service early and feed Caleb before anyone else, but this is only for him. Come with me, please."

"Oh, thank you! I hope you know I don't want special treatment. I'm sorry for all this trouble but extremely grateful. I've been desperate for him to be able to eat."

Susan with Caleb in tow eagerly followed the man to a place he proudly announced had been prepared just for the two of them. With a flourish he pulled the chair back for her.

She was trying not to cry, trying not to give in to overwhelming emotions. Her back was killing her from walking all day in the dreadful heels, and she couldn't take one more night of not being able to give her baby what he needed. Although her eyes were blurred with tears, she noticed the place set for her had been beautifully decorated with much love. There was a centerpiece with artificial flowers and an array of bowls and dishes, along with two pieces of lemon meringue pie. The fanciest, birthday cake discards of the day had been placed alongside. It was a meal that a grown man couldn't finish.

"This is just for us?" Dumbfounded, Susan looked at the

man holding her chair.

"This..." he paused with a big grin, "we are calling the family table."

The men served Susan and her toddler as if they were guests in the finest restaurant. Caleb took a few bites of beans, a bite of cottage cheese, and then promptly fell asleep in his pie. Susan tenderly picked him up, wiped the meringue off his cheek, and rocked him in her arms. The snoring toddler never heard the men file noisily into the room, shouting and pushing one another. He never saw his mother lower her head with shame over the top of his, nor would he ever know how much she worried the hardened men would resent her for the special treatment.

After the meal when the men filed out to line up for showers, Susan quietly slipped out of the room with her boys and Glenn followed.

"I have to quit coming in late," Glenn said as they stepped out into the courtyard, the coolness of the evening causing Susan to hug Caleb close. Not a breeze was stirring, but the men were filling the air with the smell of cigarettes as they stood around the coffee can ashtrays placed around the perimeter.

"Kevin has been nice about it, but I was hired to open up in the mornings and I can't face him day after day like this. I'm afraid they're going to ask me to leave." Balancing plates and cartons, he had stopped at the rear door of the car and began setting them down in the back seat. He then reached over and took the sleeping boy from his mother and laid him in the car. Kelly jumped through the open door, clutching his bag of sweet treasures.

Glenn waited until they were all in the car. "I want to talk to you before we get back to the kids."

Apprehensively, she looked over at him in the darkened vehicle. The street light reflected off his face displaying the gravity of the moment. He didn't say anything for a while, clearly struggling.

"Honey, I've been thinking a lot about something." His next words were almost a whisper. "I think we should go on the streets."

Frightened, Susan saw that he meant it. "Are you sure we can't just use Pat's raft," she tried one more time, hoping he still might be able to envision the idea.

"No! I don't want to hear about that again! Suzi, the girls aren't even with us most of the time. They beg to stay at Jennifer and Adolph's house more and more. They can't stand being out in the water, and this family needs to all be together. We can go out on the boat on weekends...when I don't have to get to work on time."

Susan turned to stare out her window, stare at the men standing around in circles, smoking and laughing. They have nothing to be happy about she thought. They have cigarettes to smoke after a free shower and then it's in the bushes for them. She sat slowly shaking her head. Suddenly gripped by an old fear coming back from the shadows, she knew, this time, there would be no escape. There would be no reprieve. She resigned herself to face the danger.

"I know it's risky but we have to keep my job." He had wanted to encourage, but even in the dark his face mirrored the defeat he was feeling.

"Okay," she said after several moments. "We'll go on the streets then."

The short ride back was silent, but back inside the bus a few minutes later the couple's sales campaign was meeting with firm resistance.

"You guys are crazy!" Holly fumed. "I don't want to live in a bus. I don't want my friends to find out I live in a bus. Where are you going to park it?"

The twelve-year-old had just been informed she could now sleep in her own little room. This could be the first night because they had decided they were going to stay in the bus.

"You didn't like the boat either, Holly." Her mother calmly tried to reason. "What should we do?"

"No, I don't like the boat. I hate it! I'm sick the whole time, and when we come in I stay sick for hours. I want a house! I want a house like normal people. Why won't you do that? Why do you want to live like weirded-out gypsies or something?" Holly railed. "Normal parents want to live in houses."

"We want a house too, Holly, more than you." Susan felt Glenn's wounding even before her eyes caught his reaction. The darts had pierced him through.

Eyes returned to focus on the children assembled before her. "We've been on the housing list for two years. We don't make enough money to get a house and feed you guys too. No one is going to rescue us, so it's up to us to take care of ourselves."

She peeked at Glenn again and saw his slumped shoulders, saw the despair as he held his head, staring at the floor.

"Until they come and take all of you kids away because they don't like how we are doing the job, then Dad and I are going to keep right on doing the best we know."

Jackie had been quiet during her sister's tirade. "I think it's cool staying inside. Is it legal?" she asked.

"No, it's not legal," her mother answered quietly. If the

police come, I want everyone to be quiet and let Dad and I handle it." Susan caught the look on Jason's face change as his expression turned hard. She knew he would hate being in any compromising position and knew how he would disapprove of this. The kids had always been taught to respect authority and obey the laws of the land, but now they were struggling to find some they could obey.

"Not legal?" Holly was outraged.

"No, it's not legal." Susan was losing patience and fighting to control what she might say.

"Why don't you go to where it is legal then?" She yelled at her mother with frustration. She also appeared frightened.

"Because, Holly, we can't be legal anywhere! That's why we went to all of the trouble to go out into the middle of the ocean. It's against the law to be homeless here, the same as it was all the other places where we were homeless. The difference here is we can always take you guys somewhere to get you something to eat. Beans at the mission are better than the nothing we've had in the past."

"Yeah, and we get lots of stale doughnuts. Don't forget about that little bonus," Jason piped up sarcastically. Then he chuckled. It was a bonus and a real one at that.

He had good reason to be honestly thankful, having horrible memories of nearly starving in the past, memories of secretly sharing his food ration with his sisters. Hunger hurt, and he hadn't wanted them to suffer as much as he was. The ravenous little creatures had quickly gobbled up the nightly macaroni and canned peas from the church basket. There were too many nights of real hunger after working hard all day simply to keep their house. His mother had caught on to what he was doing and put a stop to it, but not in time. It had taken a visit to the emergency room and then a call from a very angry doctor before the emergency food stamps were released. Susan didn't want to remember anymore, but knew Jason would never forget.

"And I thank God that there is an ocean right here we can escape to, that allows us to be legal!" Susan could feel herself losing control. She let loose with a torrent of angry words. "The ocean is unacceptable to you, and the bus is unacceptable to you. We are unacceptable to you, but we are the parents that God gave you. We may be poor, but that doesn't make us bad!"

There was an awkward silence. This was not the mother they knew.

Susan stared at her daughter. "You are stuck with us, legal or not, so you had better decide to make the best of it."

The tired mother looked helplessly at the stunned family. "We can all work together, guys, or we can pull against each other, but we won't survive doing that. I don't know what is going to happen, but we have to trust the Lord. Sometimes when you're as afraid as Dad and I get there isn't anything else you can do."

No one made a sound. Wordlessly, Holly climbed into her room and shut the little Z door, hooking it with the sound of a click.

Inwardly Susan cried to the Lord. Oh Jesus, why don't they love us? We're not mean to them. We don't yell or try to hurt them. Why can't they love us? Don't they know we're trying everything we can possibly do? In a solitary prison with her thoughts she agonized over what would happen next. Her husband had made up his mind, and the conclusion was terrifying. There was no way to prepare for sleeping on the streets, hidden with five kids inside a traveling monstrosity unacceptable to the time and culture in which they lived.

Glenn fired up the bus and drove down the road. They had very little gas and no idea of where they would go. Susan stood beside him on the second step down, wanting to see out the window. Peering intently into the darkness, she looked for any indication as to where they might stay. After traveling about a mile on their journey into the new unknown they turned on Santa Barbara Street. A bit further down this road they crossed some railroad tracks, and Glenn noticed a short, adjacent side street. No houses were nearby, and it looked trashy with abandoned cars and junk lying around in a nearby vacant field.

"I wonder if this is the wrong side of the tracks?" he joked.

"Don't worry," Susan answered. "Every side is going to be wrong."

"Yeah? So let's park." He pulled the bus to the curb and turned the key off.

In the dark she began to think of several reasons why it would be a mistake to park there and mentioned them all. Her biggest fear was losing the kids. Glenn felt that too but reassured his wife that whatever would happen could just happen there, and there wasn't going to be a better place.

They climbed into bed and remained awake listening for sounds. With trepidation they waited for the dreaded high whine of a police cruiser to pull up alongside. A few feet away a train startled them, roaring by with its screaming whistle and earth-shaking vibrations rattling the bus. The spinning white light momentarily filled the interior of the bus as it passed.

"Lord," Glenn prayed, his deep voice penetrating the darkness. "Please protect us from anything that can happen. Take care of my family, please."

"Yes," added his wife. "We need to be rescued from all of this. Please don't let anything happen to the children. We need your help."

Susan awakened around 2:00 AM, suddenly alarmed. She had heard that recognizable sound, the one she feared most. Peering out the window, she watched a police cruiser slowly drive by, not even glancing back in their direction. She needed to see that. It would help to calm her increasing fears. She needed to know they could make it through just one night.

God, you're my refuge. I trust in you and I'm safe!...Fear

nothing....not flying arrows in the day, not disease that prowls

through the darkness, not disaster that erupts at high noon,...no

harm will even graze you...Yes, because God is your refuge.

Psalms 91 The Message

Crazy Man

The day had started out unremarkable. Most days were in paradise, but for the Dunns it seldom remained so. Like a scene out of Robinson Crusoe, the Dunns were stranded on an island, a piece of asphalt of their own. It was one where they found themselves stuck between two worlds. Eerily they walked around and behaved as though they should belong as always, but were increasingly regarded as alien visitors.

"Indians circling, Jason?" his mom asked, looking up from the floor where she sat drawing with the boys.

Jason glanced out of the window from his perch above. "More every day, Mom." He shook his head. "I think we are a zoo exhibit. I'm about ready to sell tickets and charge admission."

She stood and peered through the curtains, but the parade of the curious quickly caused her to retreat below the window, free from staring eyes. Sitting on the floor while the skylights bathed her in the brilliant light was cheering. It felt safe to be hidden in the light. She could pretend to be happy and normal as always.

The day continued with all the activities little boys bring into life. They went down to the rocks to look at the fish and catch crabs, and then they put homemade boats into the water. They walked to the free shuttle for the adventure of going to the library for some new picture books, coming back along the beach with the books stuffed safely in backpacks and walking barefoot along the surf's edge. It had been a good day.

Susan stood at the makeshift galley consisting of a Coleman stove tied with kite string and perched on top of an old cabinet the right height and with a durable, Formica top. She'd been stirring fried potatoes on the single burner, but was almost out of time before leaving to get Glenn. She reached down and snatched a spoonful. The smells of garlic and pepper wafting up and swirling around had enticed her to sample the unfinished product.

"I have to get Dad from work now, so be sure and keep the boys in the bus." She turned and handed the spatula to Jason. "Don't let them get near the stove. Don't let this burn. You can turn the fire down if you need to."

"I know, Mom. Everything will be fine. I can handle this, all right?" Jason reassured her, rather exasperated by the steady stream of admonitions.

"It's just that Caleb is so quick, and you know we can't let them get away, not even for a minute," she said apologetically. "The meat is ready to go in now. Remember to keep stirring the bottom."

Jumping out of the back door, she hollered a final, "I'll be right back, okay?"

Susan drove quickly through town. She was hungry and wanted to get back soon. The ride was pleasant and picking Glenn up at work for the umpteenth time was all part of the routine.

"I have the compressor already aired up for the tire, hon. We won't have to stop to do that tonight."

"Great, 'cause I'm so tired I just want to be done," Glenn mumbled. He chatted about things he still had to do before nightfall while they drove toward Ledbetter Beach. Directly in their line of sight was a swirling mixture of pinks and oranges, a panorama in the sky promising to be another gorgeous sunset. From start to finish it had taken less than thirty minutes, and they were passing through the entrance to the harbor.

While driving through the kiosk, they were spotted by a tall, lanky, homeless man known to them.

"Hey!" he shouted, throwing his arm in the air, but this was not the friendly greeting they would have expected. He was easy to recognize from a distance. His prematurely graying hair and angular face set him off. The moment he saw them, he spun around and raced to their car. As he got closer, they saw his eyes opened wide and face flushed.

"What's up, Bill? You look upset." Glenn shouted through the open window.

"I'll say!" Bill panted, slamming his large bony hands against the car. "Hey! You guys need to get back to the bus fast!" Sweat poured off his face and his voice rose. "There's someone in there holding your sons hostage, and I just now called the police!"

Out of the corner of her eye, Susan noticed several Harbor Patrols with lights flashing. They were swarming to the area where they had parked, but they seemed to be staying away from the bus itself.

"That's crazy!" she said reaching behind her and opening the back door for Bill to get in. He jumped inside but couldn't get the door shut as Glenn was already driving off.

"What's going on?" Glenn yelled back over his shoulder to Bill while stomping on the pedal, causing the back wheels to spin on the little Corvair. The car lurched forward in a burst of speed.

Bill leaned forward and shouted in Glenn's ear. "Yeah, man! It's true!" He shot a wild look at Susan. She noticed he was pale with pasty-white lips, and sweat was beading up on his forehead.

"Jason told me to get the cops quick! Some guy is holding him and the kids hostage, and he's threatening to kill him." Bill's voice rose as he spoke and his arms were punctuating the air for emphasis. His hands shook.

"Don't worry," he looked at Susan, considering the effect upon the mother of the children he was portraying as near-goners. "Jason is between the man and the boys. He's got them stashed up in the back bedroom."

Oh sure, she thought. Don't worry. Are you kidding me? Stupefied, she slowly shook her head, trying to believe this wasn't happening. Susan was petrified with fear even though Jason was as big and strong as a boy could get. He knew how to keep a cool head on his shoulders when the occasion warranted, and she thought back to previous sticky situations where he had proven himself quite capable. Knowing that wasn't helping her at the moment, however.

"Does he have a weapon that you know of?" Glenn hollered back at Bill as he brought the car to a screeching halt. In one quick move he was out of the car and heading to the bus at a run.

Bill's voice called after him, "Don't know, man. He's just threatening to kill Jason! I know that!"

Susan reached over and turned the key off. "Why is the Harbor Patrol staying away?" She looked over her shoulder at the idling vehicles staged nearby.

"Oh man, with a hostage situation they're gonna wait 'til the city cops get here," Bill answered.

Jackie, coincidentally, happened to choose this one moment in time to arrive at the bus and was fast approaching the steps. Glenn held a hand up as he hopped on the first step. "Stay outside and out of my way," he barked.

Curious, she mouthed an expression and gestured to her mother as if to ask what was going on. She had expected a friendly greeting and not this sharp reaction from her father, especially after not seeing him all day. Susan shook her head, putting a finger to her mouth in a sign to remain quiet, then slipped out of the car and stood beside her daughter. She hopped up on the front bumper, stretching her hands over the hood for balance, and stood on tip-toes to peer through the front window. She had to see what was going to happen.

"Mom?" Jackie was scared.

"Shh!" Susan turned her head away, her attention fixating on the sights and sounds from within. She watched Glenn walk up to the ragged looking man deep inside the bus. The skylights beamed the sunlight overhead like a theater floodlight. It sparkled and danced, surrounding the surreal stage below with false cheerfulness. She saw clearly until Glenn's steady approach to the rear blocked the unfolding scenario, but her first view of the stranger showed him with a small, pointed-shaped head and a dirty mop of brown, shaggy hair which appeared to be sliding off the back of him. Pictures came to her mind of imaginary Neanderthal men she had seen in books. Huge, shaggy eyebrows, unshaven, small skull, jutted forward jaw...oh yes, the resemblance was uncanny.

"Hey, buddy. What's happening here?" Glenn spoke loud but calmly while walking toward him. Glenn's body filled the narrow bus aisle, effectively preventing any further viewing by his wife. She managed to catch a glimpse of a very worried Jason pointing sharply at the boys to stay put. They were in the loft, perched at the little doorway entrance, and poised to jump down at any second. His threatening

69

stare held them at bay, but it seemed that it would only be moments before their instincts to pounce would overtake. Whenever their daddy came through the door, that was the signal to attack joyfully the legs of the one they loved so much. Unable to differentiate between the seriousness of the situation or understand the threat, they were ready to override the sternness of big brother for what they knew was the most glorious moment of their day. Susan had seen the joy in their faces bubbling up like a volcano that would not be contained by any warning, and she immediately realized how dangerous this present moment was.

"I ain't leaving this house until I git my wallet!" A deep voice bellowed from inside. "This man stole my wallet out of my backpack!" The crazed man turned toward Jason, his tone menacing and loud, "And I'm gonna kill him if he doesn't give it back!"

"No, you are not going to kill him. This is not a house, and my son did not take your money. He would never take your money. You didn't leave a backpack here before, mister. You don't even know my son."

The man rambled on in some gibberish Susan couldn't comprehend. Extremely befuddled, he mumbled to himself. Once again he demanded Jason return his wallet.

"I was here before in this house, and that's when you took it out of my backpack."

Jason glared fiercely and steadily at the man. In a quiet voice, he said, "Remember, you came to the door and asked for matches? I walked back in to get you some."

He glanced at his dad and started talking to him but kept his eyes on the intruder. "Dad, he followed me inside and started accusing me of taking his wallet. He started threatening, and I grabbed the boys and threw them up top

70

to get them away from him. I just happened to see Bill walking by outside, so I yelled for help."

"You're not gonna get away with this!" The man shouted, his eyes pinning Jay.

"Look, mister," Jason said, his voice rising. "You've never been in this house before because this is not a house. It's a bus...an old school bus! Don't you see the windows next to where the seats used to be? Don't you see the green walls, the insides of a school bus? Look at the red, rubber, floor aisle down the center. It's still there. Ever been in a school bus before?"

There was a brief pause as if this new information was being considered. "Well, I ain't leaving," the man stubbornly declared.

Looking through the front windshield from her outside perch, Susan watched Glenn quickly grab the guy by the neck with one hand and spin him around by the shoulder with the other.

"Yes, my friend. You are going to leave." Glenn had deftly moved behind him and was now between the boys and the visitor. Pushing him toward the front of the bus, he continued, "You are going to leave right now."

Once at the door, the intruder was spun around again, and Glenn threw several body punches, then an uppercut to the face. During the quick moments of the scuffle, the surprised man fell into the windshield, cracking it severely.

When she saw the men coming her way, Susan immediately jumped down and went to grab Jackie from the door. She almost didn't pull her away in time before Glenn grabbed and kicked him out the door. Blood spurted from his nose and dribbled down the front of his torn and dirty, black sweatshirt. He stumbled and fell hard onto the asphalt.

Susan and Jackie stared at the man who had plopped right at their feet.

He scrambled to get up, yelling as the blood poured from his face. "Help! Call 911! Somebody help me!" He struggled to stay on his feet and staggered away toward the marina bathrooms.

Instantly, mom and daughter were in the bus, the man forgotten. "Are you okay, Jason? Are you okay, boys?" She searched their faces.

"What happened?" Jackie asked, mystified.

"I'm okay, but I was worried that these two," Jason looked up and shook his head at some wide-eyed but cheerful little guys who remained oblivious,"...these two were gonna jump down any second, and I would have to fight that guy with the boys in the middle."

"Daddy!" They had waited long enough. They leaped toward their dad's waiting arms for the shenanigans to begin. "Daddy!" they shouted again.

"My baby boys!" Glenn spoke with a high baby voice. He loved to talk to them that way. He hugged them both at once. "My little men. You were so good. I am very proud of you. I am proud of all my boys." He looked at Jason. "You did good, son. You did real good."

"But Daddy," Caleb interrupted, frowning. "Why did you hafta hit dat man fo'?"

"Yeah, Dad," Kelly chimed in. "Oh man, you got him good. You went pow, pow, pow!" he said while mimicking with his fists." Clearly he was impressed, whatever Dad's reasons were.

"Well, boys, I had to make sure he wasn't going to do anything because your mama and your sister..." he glanced sternly but playfully at his wife, "were standing right over

72

where that man was. You wouldn't want anything to happen to your mama, would you?"

Both boys with serious looks on their faces nodded. No, they would not want that.

"Well, don't worry. I didn't hurt him. Just a few body blows to soften him up. My girls were standing right where he had to go." Glenn cocked his head and looked toward his wife and daughter. "My girls just had to be right there to see what was happening...right at the doorway." He smiled a little and shook his head, visibly a bit exasperated with his girls. "Had to make sure nothing would happen to them." He looked back at the boys and smiled. Their little eyes were glowing, the reflected sunlight bouncing off their faces. They nodded in agreement. Dad was clearly their hero.

"He will be all right," he continued, "and my baby boys are safe." He continued to speak with his high, cheerful voice. "I am never going to let anything happen to my boys, or mama, or sister. Ain't that right, Jason?"

"Nope," Jason smirked. "Not as long as I'm here." He was beginning to relax, and everything had ended well after the tense moments. He was still a bit white but knew he had handled things masterfully. He was also proud of his dad.

Both boys let loose, apparently with some secret signal, and jumped on their father. The monkey wrestling had begun. They were whooping and hollering, and hugs were going on with everyone.

Bill popped his head inside the door. "Hey, the cops are out here wanting to talk to you, Glenn. Is everybody all right in here?" He had to have noticed all the laughter and play going on, but it had been terrifying only moments before. More reassurance was necessary.

"Boys, you stay here with your brother. I have to go talk to some men right now, but I'll be right back." Caleb wasn't letting go. He was wrapped around a leg and was clinging on better than a dryer sheet sticking to a blanket.

"Cabey, let go." His dad tried to pull him off as he kept moving forward. "Daddy has to talk to the nice policeman. I be right back, I promise."

Susan reached over and peeled the strong little arms off so Glenn could make his getaway. Caleb held tight with his legs locked around, making his dad pull his leg up to escape his son's determination.

"Pwaw-mis, Daddy?" Caleb called after him.

"Yes, I will be right back and then we will play."

A Harbor Patrol officer stood outside the bus door with his report book out and was writing something in it. "Had some trouble here I see."

Glenn began to explain the previous moments and exactly what occurred to cause the windshield to meet its demise. He was feeling great relief and was his usual cordial and jovial self, the one who always had everything in control. He retold everything without the panic everyone had felt, and it seemed there was now no problem at all.

The officer listened with head down while writing furiously on his pad, trying to get it all down, until a call caused him to excuse himself. He reached up and tapped the radio on his shoulder. He began to smile, turning and staring over at the marina while listening intently. He chuckled as he clicked the off button and returned to the writing business at hand.

"Your attacker is over at the phone booth right now calling 911. He is asking for medical assistance and protection from you. Says you attacked him." He chuckled again. "Well, I need to inform you that you have the right to press charges against this individual, and we can get medical attention for your family just to make sure everyone is all right."

The blond young man put his pen down and looked at Glenn. "You have the right to defend yourselves, and it is obvious you only used enough force to subdue the assailant and gain control on behalf of your family's welfare. There was no intent on your part to cause him any serious harm or take revenge. You operated well within the law." The officer paused, looking away for a moment. When he looked back, he said, "I might mention it was a job very well done. My hat is off to you, sir."

The bleep-bleep of a nearby ambulance punctuated the air, and the circling red light flashed throughout the parking lot in the deepening sunset shadows. Staging until the outcome, they had been like vultures waiting for carrion, and now quickly made their way over to the marina.

"Well, thank you, officer. I don't think he even knows who we are or will remember anything after he comes down off his high. I don't believe we will be in any more danger. Nobody is hurt, and my son took care of things like a champion. We don't need medical attention. It was my friend, Bill, who called you, and I am very grateful for him doing that. Thank you for responding, but I don't want to press charges. He has enough problems already."

"Are you sure?" The officer didn't seem surprised or bothered by Glenn's decision. Perhaps he thought justice had already been served. "I rather agree with you that he is harmless right now. He's crying like a baby for us to help him." He struggled to hold back his chuckle.

"They have already assessed nothing is wrong with him, but they will take him anyway at his insistence. Sorry about your windshield. If you need us, please call again."

Susan had been standing at the door listening, but now had to know the answer to something that was bothering her. "Why didn't you come and rescue the kids when you first got the call? I saw so many patrol cars before we got here. All the officers were sitting in their cars and away from the bus, but no one was getting out. How come?"

"I'm sorry. We can't do anything in a hostage situation. We have to get city for that. We had to wait until they came and took control of the situation. They are with him now. These are the rules we have to go by, but your husband handled everything about as well as anyone could. I am glad it worked out for all of you. Enjoy your day." He tipped his hat at Glenn as he folded the clipboard under his arm. Glenn reached out and shook his hand.

"Thanks again, man."

The smiling cop nodded as he entered his car and left. This was going to be a story to share and remember. Relief was palpable.

Back in the bus, everyone, excited and happy, was talking at once. The offender would later be seen on occasion walking around town, but he never recognized any of them again, a total lost soul vacant of meaning. He was like many others they'd meet, getting little from his gift of life.

There never would be extra money for the windshield, and the packing tape would continue to hold all the huge cracks together. It would keep out most of the wind and rain. It would hold together for years. Because the bus had a split windshield they would be told it was not legally necessary to replace the passenger side. The law was not violated, so the tape remained.

A short while after the commotion died down that day and all was returning to calm, Holly arrived back home. She stepped innocently into the bus, stunned to be greeted loudly by her sister. "Holly!" Jackie shouted. "You missed everything!"

The people who walk in darkness will see a great light. For those who live in a land of deep darkness, a light will shine.

Isaiah 9:2 New Living Translation

...By Candlelight

Cold winds were blowing in the damp, rainy night. The roof leaked in a multitude of spots and pots, cups, and buckets were placed strategically to catch some of it. The Coleman stove spit a little heat into the atmosphere, but otherwise could not alleviate a sure prescription for depression.

"Mom, my clean clothes are all wet. This stupid can fell over and I didn't know it."

"We will hang them and they will be okay. Hand them to me for now," Mom answered.

"Mom, my blanket is wet."

"That's because you pee the bed, said a small instigator.

"Shut-up Kelly! It's from the leaky bus and you know it."

"Kelly, that's enough. You know how you would feel if someone talked to you that way. Remember the golden rule."

She grabbed the offending blanket and hung it over the long bar used to open the door. "I have another blanket you can use. Don't worry."

Susan was putting up a valiant fight but was steadily losing ground to the forces threatening to destroy. Sitting in the darkness listening to the drip, drip, drip of invading dampness was the worst. Caulk hadn't worked, and they didn't know where all the leaks were coming from. The skylights which permitted so much joy in the sunshine were apparently leaky sieves bringing in wet despair during the rain.

She thought back to times past when they had lived in a small RV. Nights before had all been filled with peace, joy, and the noisy squeals of little ones playing cars or planes on the postage-stamp sized floor. Quiet coloring in books or the hustle and bustle of doll life was cramped, but not an unpleasant experience. It had always been taken for granted the mom would cook, the kids would play with Dad while waiting, and later everyone would help with dishes. None of that was possible now.

There were many shocks with this strange twist in their lives. The difficulty with getting showers, the unsettling need to hide one's existence, not being able to stay dry or see anything in the dark were all new. These were severe and extreme in themselves, but the addition of the Anne Frank lifestyle brought with it a dismal sadness. One never knew when the fatal knock on the door would come, bringing with it the authorities and the full force of the law against the vulnerable refugees.

Outside, the throaty sound of the little Corvair pulled up announcing Dad was home. Always an occasion for celebration, the little boys jumped and shouted, "Daddy! Yea! Daddy's here!"

Jason slid open the door of his front loft and peered out. He nodded a cursory greeting, and Jackie peeked around her corner to say hi.

Glenn was carrying a large bag under his arm. He reached down and managed to scoop up two boys, hugging them with the other arm.

Looking at his wife he announced, "We won't be in the dark tonight, Suzi!"

She tried to remember the last time she had seen him this

excited. Curious, she looked down and watched as he began pulling out long, white candles one after another from the dirty, green, canvas bag he had tossed to the floor.

"There is a place at work where they have me store all the used candles after they do a wedding." He had begun to light one after the other, placing them in groups of two or three and sticking them on every dish he could find. He would first pour a little wax from a lit candle onto the plate where it would cool quickly, allowing it to become the glue holding the beautiful slender tapers in place. The walls began to glow. Glenn continued pulling out candles and lighting them until more than three dozen were blazing all over the bus. No dark corner was safe from their brilliance.

"It's beautiful," Susan finally spoke, mesmerized by the gorgeous hues reflected in the wood and the flickering of the lights. "Where did you say you got all of these?"

"They are kept in a large bin, and Suzi," he started laughing uncontrollably, "he, he, he, he..." His laugh made other people laugh just to hear it. "Suzi," he said again when he finally caught his breath, "they've been storing them for years and years! There is a ton of them in there, and they are all barely used. Every wedding needs new candles, so they can't do anything with them. We will never run out! The Lord said let there be light." Glenn started laughing again. "He, he, he, he...and we got light, baby!" His face lit up with pure joy as he surveyed his family basking in the warm glow of simple light. He grabbed a couple of mirror tiles and placed them behind the candles, reflecting and magnifying the candlepower.

"Did you get permission? I mean did you ask anyone if you could have them?" She could see on his face that he had not. "Maybe we could offer to buy them."

"Oh, Suzi, there are so many, and no one cares about them. If I thought they did, I would ask them about the candles."

She was not so sure, but with the darkness finally gone it was harder to feel the need to request authorization for the blessed things. The dismal cloud hanging over them for so long was slipping away. It slowly receded past the walls and out into the night. Home felt more like a safe place, and a cheerful atmosphere returned reclaiming its residence.

Kelly and Caleb sat melting wax from a candle each held, allowing it to become putty in their fingers. Kelly began to build a little wax sculpture from his drippings.

"Hot!" Caleb dropped his candle on the steel floor, and it rolled a few inches. He put his thumb in his mouth and sucked on it. Tears welled up threatening to spill over.

"Don't get so close, Cabey. You will get burned," Kelly admonished. "Here, do this. Watch." Kelly let a little wax drop, waiting a moment for it to cool and then gingerly tested it with his finger. "See how I do it? You do it like this and you won't get burned."

Caleb, watching intently, took his thumb out of his mouth and said, "Oh, okay. Caywub can do it. Watch me do it, Kellwie." Looking up at his mom, he announced, "Look, Mommy. Can do it. Kellwie showed me how to make wax."

"Yes, honey, you can." The face looking at him was softer and more relaxed. "You be careful with fire, and you won't get burned. Fire is dangerous. It can hurt you." A few moments later she added, "But it is also nice...very nice."

Jason stuck his feet out of the door of his cubicle, letting them hang while he sat smiling at everyone. "It is getting warm up here. Yessiree, nice and toasty. I have at least a dozen going in my room right now."

"I want some in my room," Holly piped up.

"Yeah, me too," said Jackie.

"Wait a minute," their mother said. "You guys can burn the bus down. It is made of wood, remember? No one is taking candles anywhere unless I can see them. No one except Jason."

"Yeah, when I was a little kid I used to be a pyro, but I got the Mom cure. I am very careful of fire now. But..." his smile grew, "I still like fire." Jason popped back into his cubbyhole and lay staring at the flickering glow.

"I feel like we are wasting them by using so many at a time, and yet...I don't care. It is so pretty."

"Waste them. I will bring home this many every night. We will never run out."

They sat for a long time watching them slowly burn. They sat and talked like before entertaining some new dreams while burying a few old. They gazed at the flickers until the children grew quiet. They were tired too and still had to face the uncertainty of the night, but mostly they were thankful— thankful just for light.

Be submissive to every human institution and authority for the sake of the Lord, whether it be to the emperor as supreme, Or to governors as sent by him to bring vengeance (punishment, justice) to those who do wrong and to encourage those who do good service.

1 Peter 2:13-14 Greek Amplified Bible

Don't Go In There!

Cantankerous as always, the old bus was exceedingly difficult to coax into its daily mile-and-a-half journey from the railroad tracks to the beach. In the land of eternally perfect weather, one could not blame the cold for the onerous motor being nearly impossible to start nor could the heat be blamed for the gauges instantly registering warm. Once started, it would chug pitifully down the street threatening to cough and die at any moment. Glenn would need to pump the gas pedal furiously while at the same time gear up or down, his hand clenched tightly on the Allison knob at his side. The engine required his best efforts to be fooled into staying alive for the early morning run.

The kiosk at the harbor entrance had a mandatory stop which always caused the tired thing to lose momentum. Without fail, it would immediately cough and sputter its last, causing them to have to coast into the closest parking space. This motor death going into "port" was advantageous for one reason alone. The brakes barely worked, and the coast was the final thing which stopped the beast entirely. Sometimes it stopped a bit short of making it in, and the worried couple could only hope everyone would think they weren't good at parking. It would be a few hours before the limping along could begin anew as the engine would not be able to be started, and so the landing had to be good.

Glenn smiled and waved friendly greetings to all the happy people who stopped to stare at the big, wooden crate lumbering in. A group of Dunns stared back from inside, peering intently to see if their leader would be able to find and drift into two empty spaces side by side, along with a third in the forefront, the necessary combination required to park safely. None of the friendly faces would ever guess how serious was the praying from the group inside.

"Go, go, go, go," was heard from the rear as the two little ones cheered the wheels on a bit further.

"Yaaay! Perfect!" came a chorus of cheers.

"Thank you, Jesus! Good job, Dad."

"Another day safely home," breathed Susan with a sigh. She noticed a couple of harbor patrol officers standing in front of the Marina restrooms and waved. "That's the guy you were talking to before." Glenn looked over and waved too. "He seemed really nice. I think he might help us figure out a better plan. Remember, he was considering allowing us to park by the boat trailers, and he said he was going to work on it?"

"That would be good," Glenn said, hopping off the bus. "I'll be right back. I'm going to use the restroom before I blast off for work. Today I'll be early for a change. Kevin will be surprised, eh?"

Four adult bodies and two squirmy short ones all danced around one another in the narrow aisle while attempting early morning activities. Similar to a dance in a moving Twister game, all were stumbling over the same set of points in space. At the moment, most of this centered on sharing the solitary, two-foot, square mirror.

"Get out of the mirror, Jackie. You don't need to be any more beautiful."

"Hey, I can pop your little blond head off if you keep putting it in my way." She grabbed his head and jaw with her hands and pretended to shake it gently back and forth.

This made Kelly giggle.

"Whoa, I better get outta here," he said, ducking under her grasp.

"Move over. We can both fit," Holly said, poking her head in.

"I have a class to get to, you guys. I actually need this," chimed in Jason. He popped his head into view just over the top of theirs. "Wow! Three actually fit."

"I wanna see." Caleb pushed against legs, staring up at the snug-fitting group.

"Come here. You're all beautiful enough," interrupted their mother. "Time to get your breakfast." Susan glanced out toward the parking lot just then and noticed a wide-eyed Glenn storming to the bus. His face was bright red, and his jaw was clenched in rage.

"Uh, oh, guys. Something is wrong. Something is very wrong," she warned.

Glenn reached out, grabbed the doors, and ripped them open, smacking them against the inside wall. "I can't believe what just happened!" he yelled with white-lipped fury as he stomped up the stairs. His eyes were bloodshot red. "He gave me a ticket for using my boat card just to use the bathroom."

Susan dropped the pan onto the stove, breakfast forgotten. "He can't do that, can he? All the boat owners told us there would be no problem. You were with me, Glenn, when I asked them the rules." She shook her head in disbelief. "Remember, we were told all the mooring people were treated the same as slip owners?"

"Go tell your friendly Mr. Harbor cop. Here is the ticket!" He threw it on the counter. "Add this to the list of the other things we can't pay for!" Glenn's voice had risen to a shout.

"Rick said he has lived here for years. This is wrong!" Jason exploded. "He said there are many who have lived here for years." His face flushed with the full impact of the injustice. "Rick said as long as we keep bringing the boat in on a regular basis...and we have. We bring it in for as long as they will let us. What more can we do?"

Susan couldn't take her eyes off of the ticket and stared at it as though it was a conquering foreign invader. In essence, it was. The authorities they had gone to for help had just become their betrayers, and the little piece of paper was tangible proof. They had been vulnerable and fragile, and in their naivety had placed their trust in those who had authority over them. It had been foolishness to share their plight with them honestly, and now, suddenly the illusion was gone. Poof! Gone by the traitor who wore a badge.

Susan knew her husband well. He could not tolerate breaking the law or offending authorities. Not ever. As a couple, they were well aware everything they were doing was extreme, even ludicrous, but they were doing all of it to insure they were complying with the law. Everything! It was mandatory they follow all ordinances and rules in the culture they found themselves living. In their years of married life there had been a never-ending cycle of disasters threatening them with extinction, and they had been steadily squeezed from one corner of desperation into another. Yes, Susan knew her husband well, and his identity revolved around a testimony of escaping a life of crime and discovering a brand new life in Christ. He was forever grateful to be able to remain on the right side of the law since his conversion many years previous.

There was a time when they were living in Taft and work was slow during one long winter. There was enough to make the house payment but not much else. The meager food rations the church gave them were quickly consumed. Glenn had called his sister to say he was ready to send her the kids so they wouldn't starve, and Jason had been taken to the hospital, sick, weak, and hungry. Susan had thought of going to the police and telling them they were hungry and in serious trouble. Maybe they would know of another church that would give them food. Then, a more sinister plan began to form in her mind. Susan remembered hearing her husband's stories of how he used to open coke machines and steal money. She didn't have the courage to suggest it, but maybe something could be said that would cause him to think of it himself. It could be their rescue. She would never forget when she had turned on her best friend and mate with a searing indictment, "Glenn, your baby is hungry."

Glenn had looked at her like she stabbed him with a knife. He threw his hands up in the air and cried out, "What do you want me to do, Suzi? Steal?"

Yes. She was thinking exactly that. Her husband should forsake all and go steal for them so they could eat. Shocked, she stood there staring at the tears in his eyes. What had she been thinking?

"I could never steal," he continued. "I left all that behind."

The next day emergency food stamps finally arrived. They had been delayed, but Susan learned who her husband truly was. And now she was watching him crumble before her eyes like so much broken clay.

"I'd like to blow them up!" A string of words the children had never heard burst from him. "Set this whole place on fire!" The dad who never swore cut loose loudly as he paced in the tiny area near the steps. He slammed his fist on the counter. "I'd like to beat him up, the lousy, no good..."

Susan grabbed two shocked little boys standing beside her

in a fierce hug, covering one of each of their ears with one hand while holding them close to her body in an attempt to deafen the other.

"Glenn!" she spoke sharply. "We don't cuss in this family. You don't either."

Glenn ignored her. "I bet he wouldn't last two minutes with me. I'm through with this, Suzi! I'm not playing their sick game!"

Shocked, scrunched little faces looked up at their father spouting the ugly words.

"How can they do that to us?" Jackie cried, tears falling down her face. "We're just kids, Dad, and you don't break any laws! You just go to work all the time. Mom, it's not like we're selling drugs or anything. Why do they want to hurt us?" Her lip was trembling and her face contorted, unable to comprehend the cruelty of the ones she had been taught were her "friends".

"What do they expect us to do?" Holly's words dripped with acid, "Go drown so they can keep the harbor beautiful and kid free?" Gotta keep Santa Barbara perfect!" She spit each word out with venom. "Can't have families running a muck, especially not homeless ones."

"I'd like to see them blow up, too," said Jason. "Maybe a little something under the hood of their cars, eh?"

"What?" Susan shook her head and turned to stare at her son, "No!" She was still trying to figure out damage control for her husband's swearing when all the kids started coming unglued and exploding with a rage she had never witnessed before. She absolutely could not fathom her son behaving this way. Not Jason. He was always the steady one no matter what was going on. This can't be happening she thought.

"No! Stop!" she yelled, but it was as if she were invisible.

"They want to rob from the poor. Maybe we should give them some real trouble, eh Dad?" Jason ranted on, ignoring his mother.

"You got that right." Glenn cursed with a maniacal laugh. "Blow those precious toilets right out of the building!"

Jason laughed. "Make them use the free one with everyone else. Wouldn't that be great? No showers for us, no showers for anyone. Free shower zone."

"What? We can't get showers anymore?" A shocked Jackie looked first at her brother's face and then her dad's to see if it was true, and then started crying harder.

Caleb came and sat beside her on the bed.

He started to pat her on the shoulder. "Those are bad guys. Bad, bad guys. Don't cwy Jackie. It's gonna be okay." Don't werwie, Daddy." Big tears were streaking down his face.

"I hate those lousy cops!" Kelly said.

"No! Stop!" Susan tried again. "Everybody, stop! We can't act like this. God doesn't want us to be like this. What is happening to you, honey?" She searched her husband's face desperately. "Don't let them do this to you."

"You stop, Suzi!" He stared at her with a cold, dead look. "They did it! And they did it to the ones I love. Look at the ones I love. Look what is happening to them. Listen to their hurt. They did that. Why shouldn't I blow them up?"

"I don't care what anybody does to us. We can't act like this or say these things," she said sternly.

"Going to work. See you later." With no kisses goodbye and not another word, he slammed out. He drove the car recklessly and loudly, daring someone to do something. No one did. They had all left.

"Everyone, I know this is terrible. Daddy didn't mean to

say those words. We are all hurt, but we will stay together. We will get through this. Jesus will never leave us or forsake us." She glared at her son.

He immediately turned away and gathered his books. "Late for class. See you later, Mom."

Susan strapped the life vests on the boys, and they started out for their morning walk. They stopped to use the free bathrooms at Marina Three, then Susan let the boys run ahead as usual while she strolled along the boardwalk. She wanted to go somewhere and cry, but that wasn't going to be an option. She had stopped at the railings briefly, staring down at a crab crawling across the rocks below, when she heard a commotion going on in the direction of the boys. Her small son grabbed a lady's arm and hung on tightly.

"No, don't go in dare!" he cried. "Men will come and they will wobb you. They will take yo' money if you go in dare. I'm telling you the twoof." His voice got louder as he begged, "Pwease don't go in dare!"

Perplexed and interested passers-by were beginning to pause, and a crowd was forming as her older son attempted to explain his little brother's strange behavior. "The police will give you a ticket if you use this bathroom. They gave my dad one this morning, and we have a boat and a boat card and everything. Don't use this bathroom anymore or you will get one too. Come on, Caleb. There's Mom." He grabbed his brother's hand and pulled him to his stunned mother now standing as a member of the crowd and stupefied at the words coming from her young sons.

"It's okay, Caleb." Susan tried to think of how she could help to make sense of this. "The people will be fine. The police are gone now."

"Yeah," Caleb said with short gasping breaths. He looked

around furtively. "But they might come back." He started to cry. "We have to help the people...all the people, Mommy."

He hadn't lived long enough to take on all the responsibility to make sure no one would get hurt, but he was. He wasn't going to permit anything again like he just saw happen to his daddy. Three years old and barely potty-trained at night, it baffled her to understand how this could come from such a small child. She hugged him until he was able to calm down a little bit, and then she promised her baby she wouldn't let anyone hurt them. She promised they would figure everything out and told him he didn't need to worry about the people. The people would be okay. Then she walked them back to the bus to hide inside.

The curtains were closed that day, and that's how they would remain. The light continued to shine, bringing heavenly peace through the skylights, but the windows would never share again. Eyes from inside the bus would peek through the curtains at the constant surveillance from the harbor patrols circling the lots. There were no more friendly waves. The hunted refugees went without showers, went without using their boat cards, and they watched all the others use theirs. They would be paid a special visit by the director of the harbor, presenting them with a piece of paper conveniently hi-lighted in yellow and displaying the legal code regarding the use of the harbor. Unfriendly, abrupt, and cold, he seemed to be making certain they knew how unwanted they were. Susan returned his manner in kind but did thank him politely for the information.

"There they go again," scowled Jason as he peeked through the curtains. "Old baldy is out trying to catch some more illegal bathroom users."

"Let it go, Jason," implored his mother. "Please. They patrol everyone, not just us." But the paranoia permeated every member of the family. They spent family time venting rage at the so-called enemy.

"Why do they keep bothering us?" Jackie shouted angrily, pulling herself away from looking through the black curtains. "What do we do that is so terrible?"

"We exist," Susan answered. "Therein lies all the problem. It's nothing personal, guys. It's just the devil, and he has always hounded us. It's taken a new form. That's all. What we are experiencing is what the Bible calls persecution. Apostle Paul called this light affliction—just a little light affliction.

We are troubled on every side, yet not distressed; we are perplexed, but not in despair; Persecuted, but not forsaken; cast down, but not destroyed; Always bearing about in the body the dying of the Lord Jesus, that the life also of Jesus might be made manifest in our body.

2 Corinthians 4:8-10 King James Version Holy Bible

Let's See You Praise the Lord This Time!

Another day, she thought, peering through the windshield at the fading sun. "And with just the right amount of disasters to attend to," she whispered cynically under her breath. After rounding the first bend right outside the harbor parking lot, a dragging and screeching sound of scraping metal convinced Susan she was leaving engine parts all over the road. Something coming apart from underneath her vehicle caused her to stop in the road suddenly. There was no emergency lane to pull over in, and she was caught on a dangerous curve. Cars would not be able to see her until they were only a few yards behind.

"Great," she muttered. "Just great. Caleb! Kelly!" she barked crisply. "You guys stay seated, you hear me? I'll be right back and I don't want you to move!" She shouted the last at them with her best I-mean-business voice and jumped from the car.

Glancing around quickly to see if any cars were coming around the bend, she ran back to look under the car. A broken tailpipe hung down sadly, bent and misshapen where it had been scraping along the pavement. A crumpled muffler lay a few yards away where it had bounced into the gutter. Susan ran over and grabbed the muffler, came back and threw it in the back seat. As she did, she happened to spy a wire coat hanger lying on the floor, so she reached over and grabbed that. Caleb was old enough to know how to unfasten his seat belt, and he was already out of it. He was more interested in seeing what his mother was doing than in worrying about what she had just said.

"Kelly!" the stressed mother shouted loudly in the direction of the boys. "Sit on your brother until I get back!"

Kelly's eyes opened wide, and a joyous expression suddenly appeared on his face. He virtually leaped across the seat in his effort to comply with his mother's request.

To the tune of a screaming, protesting, little boy, Susan ran back and crawled under the car where she began wiring up the hot tailpipe a few inches above the ground. She had visions of being squished at any moment by an oncoming car. Kelly seemed to be thoroughly enjoying his assignment. Howls and screams steadily poured out of his little brother who apparently hadn't yet succeeded in escaping. As she lay on the gravelly asphalt trying to keep her hair from getting into the oil and dirt below, she kept shooting furtive glances over her shoulder to see if each oncoming car would notice her in time. Giving a final twist to the stiff wire, she crawled out and stood up.

"Guess I get to live," she said to no one in particular. She ran forward, grabbed open the door, and jumped back into the driver's seat. Hands covered with grease, she looked quickly around for a rag or anything to clean off with. "Oh well, Lord, I guess it's enough to be thankful for the coat hanger."

Susan drove away quickly from the dangerous corner, the car making a blaring racket without a muffler, but they were now safe. The boys immediately quieted and settled back in their seats after fastening their belts.

"That's what you get," Kelly snarled at Caleb. "That's for not minding Mom." He glared threateningly at his brother. Tears were already drying, Mom was back at the wheel, and order in the world was reestablished.

Susan reflected maybe she should be thankful for more than the coat hanger. After all, she was driving at the moment and with her mechanical abilities that qualified as a miracle of sorts.

After picking up Glenn, she chatted happily with him about his day and laughed about her experience with the muffler. He felt he could easily get it back on and it wouldn't cause anymore problems. They were driving slowly and carefully, trying not to draw attention to the noisy car. When they returned to the harbor and pulled into the lot, Susan was the first to see it.

"Look, Glenn! There's a crowd at our bus!" she pointed, frightened.

"What could have happened now?" he burst out angrily. His yelling startled everyone in the car, but they were not scared as much as he. They saw Jason standing at the door with a frightened and worried expression. Rick was there also, which was odd. He avoided groups and rarely came around. Many of the new friends the family had made were standing in a huddle, all wearing the same pitying and sad looks and directing them toward the occupants of the approaching car.

Opening the door quickly, Susan cried out to the crowd, "What's wrong? What's going on?"

A pretty lady who Susan had never met stepped forward. She was blond, wearing a white visor with pink and white shorts. "Are you Holly's mom?" she asked.

"Yes," Susan answered. "Is she all right?" She looked around frantically and realized Holly was not in sight.

"Holly's been hurt," she said gently. "You need to go to Cottage Hospital right away. The ambulance just took her. She fell and hurt her head."

Noticing Susan flinch, she quickly added, "It isn't serious. It's only a cut, and she has a bump where she fell. I found her on the beach, and I've been with her until the ambulance arrived." She paused, glanced away for a moment, and then looked back at Susan. "I have a daughter Holly's age. It's real hard for girls. Holly cried and cried. She asked for you, and I held her head." Tears escaped from the kind lady's eyes and she looked down, sadly.

There was something in the way the lady was speaking, something more she was trying to say Susan could almost understand, could almost grasp. There was a little too much compassion, too much pain when she looked at Susan. If Holly's injury was not serious then why was everyone looking as though things were extremely so? It didn't add up, and this was all terribly confusing.

The trim, petite lady reached over and took Susan's hand. She continued in a soft and soothing voice, "Holly had been drinking."

"What!" Susan gasped. "Drinking? My kids have never drunk anything. We've never had alcohol in the house. She's never been around alcohol in her life, not ever! Where could she have gotten any liquor?" In shock, Susan looked desperately at the faces staring at her, trying to make sense of what she heard, trying to see if anyone knew the answers.

Jason stepped forward, handing his dad a business card. "The cop said to give you this card. You're supposed to call him right away."

"Yeah," Rick said, "and he also said the kids should be taken away. A bus was no place for kids to live in."

"Anyway," Jason shot daggers with his eyes over at Rick before continuing, "you need to call the hospital immediately so they can get permission to treat her. I'll watch the boys. Just go!" he commanded.

His parents needed him to do that. They moved into action at their son's direction. "Don't let anything else happen," his mother ordered, jumping back into the car.

"I won't. Don't worry. I'll keep 'em inside."

Rick leaned over to the open window as they were backing up. "How you gonna have a positive attitude about things this time, Suzi? I'd like to know."

"I'm praising the Lord whatever happens!" she shouted back at him defiantly as Glenn drove off.

When they got to the hospital, stunned and dazed, they were greeted by a crying Jackie. She was being held and comforted by their friends, Jennifer and Adolph. When she saw her parents, she began to wail, "I'm sorry, Mom. I'm sorry, Dad. I almost killed my sister. I almost killed Holly."

Seeing Jackie crying hysterically, Glenn and Susan both ran over and hung onto her until she could calm down enough to speak again. When she finally opened her mouth, she let go with bursts of nonstop ramblings, sobbing in between confessions.

"I never thought any of this would happen...She stole the bottles, but it was my idea, Mom...I'm the one to blame...I gave her the idea...I asked the man...he was behind the counter...I asked him to borrow matches."

Jackie took a breath and looked at each parent. She had their full attention. She began again, but more calmly. "We'd already grabbed all of them out of the little bowl, so we knew the man at the cafe would have to go in the back to get some more. The bottles were right there, and we just grabbed them and ran. Oh, we were so scared, Mom. We never stole anything before like that. We ran and ran down the beach, and we were so scared." Jackie was crying again, and this time her parents were staring at her in open-mouthed disbelief, flabbergasted by what they just heard. Glenn reached over and pulled her close.

"Racer Rabbit, you did wrong, but you didn't almost kill your sister." Her dad tried to comfort. "My poor Racer. I'm just glad you're both going to be all right. We're going to get you girls out of here. I'm getting you and McHooley out of here, and I'm going to make everything all right, do you understand?" He hugged her tightly.

Jackie's lipped trembled, and she looked up at her dad. She tried to smile through her tears, but lost it and once again began to sob uncontrollably.

"Oh, Racer. My poor Racer," he crooned. He pushed her away at arm's length momentarily, looking her in the eyes and getting her attention. He smiled. "Stealing booze?" he tried to tease. It was a way he had. It had always worked, but right now it wasn't making things better.

"Oh, Daddy. I'm so sorry. They said Holly might die." Jackie once again was inconsolable, and her wailing could be heard throughout the small building.

"No, no. Don't cry, Rabbit. Don't cry." Her dad held her tight, patting her head gently until she slowly quieted, erupting with occasional little bursts. Finally, she let loose a big sigh.

"It's going to be okay, I promise you. Daddy will make everything all better for my girls."

Holly was suffering from acute alcohol poisoning; a nurse came out and informed them. First, she had asked who they were and satisfied herself that they indeed were the parents. "She's not fully conscious. They are still trying to bring her around in the trauma room. I'm sorry you won't be able to go to her just yet." The nurse informed them kindly but firmly with her crisp professional manner. It was common for her to deliver this type of news, but for these parents, it was their first time to hear it.

They were escorted into a cubicle-sized waiting room next to the lobby. A grave-faced doctor sat them down and gently tried to explain what had happened. The child had consumed enough alcohol to take her life, but the head injury was incidental and not serious. Her stomach was being pumped, and he was confident they had caught it in time. He was recommending release to go home. Holly would live.

"I don't think my daughter has ever tasted alcohol in her life," Susan said, feeling as though she were in a trance. "Isn't there anywhere we can get help?" She begged. "She has been depressed for a long time, and now she's suicidal?" Her voice rose in disbelief. "There must be something we qualify for."

"I'm sorry," he shook his head sadly. He looked down at his clipboard. "It says here on your paperwork you don't get Medi-Cal or have insurance. The few private programs that treat adolescents cost a great deal, and if you don't have any insurance there is just no way you could afford it. This being her first time and the fact that she got so sick, we can all hope it will be a lesson to her. Maybe she won't try it again. I'm sorry I can't offer you any more than that."

Susan had grave misgivings about his words. She was reluctant to trust in optimism with her daughter's life. It was no secret to the parents that Holly had been in trouble for quite some time. After the harbor incident with the ticket, Susan had watched a dark cloud of rage and despair settle over each of the older members of the family. They were like birds all caught and trapped in a cage waiting for their day of slaughter. Holly was crying out desperately, and her

103

mother could hear her cry, but she couldn't reach her or be of any real help.

"Honey, let's go home," her mother said when they finally let her in to see her daughter. She touched her shoulder gently. "Dad and I are here, and they said in a little while we can all go home. Would you like that?"

The stark, white walls glared down at the drama unfolding below, with blinking eyes from the lights and machines hanging off the walls. They appeared to be standing guard, ready to save a steady procession of lives, and soon the bed would be remade just in time to receive another. Holly slowly turned over on the gurney. Her eyes would open no more than cracked slits. She tried peering up at her mom through the long, thick, blond hair that was all matted and wet across her face. Her eyes were puffy and bloodshot, and a large, red bump was swelling under a bandage on her forehead. The front of her hospital gown was soaked, and she was still wearing her favorite torn jeans. Sand was in her hair, and there was also sand clinging to her arms and jeans. Susan saw the blood that was still in her daughter's hair and a puke basin sat nearby to catch any more of the vile poison that had nearly snuffed a life that day.

"Mommy, oh Mommy. I love you. I'm so sorry, Mommy. I really love you. I do." Holly sobbed, her heart broken. "Yes, I want to go home." She grabbed her mother's neck and hugged her. "I want to go home now."

The nurse, kinder now and seeming less formal, began to wrap a Cottage Hospital blanket around the shoulders of the shivering kid as she helped her get down from the gurney. "Go slow. Easy now," she coaxed. She looked at the mother. "You will have to hold onto her. This will eventually go away but probably not until tomorrow."

"I want to wear this shirt," Holly announced to the nurse, her teeth chattering while she clutched the hospital gown. She stumbled over the shoes lying on the floor next to the gurney as the nurse tried to steady her. "Can I wear this home?" She looked up at the nurse. "Mine is all messed up. I don't even know where it is."

The nurse was holding a plastic bag with Holly's clothing inside. "Yes, honey. You go ahead and wear that gown home. Here is your stuff. I'm going to give it to your mom," she said as she handed it over to the worried mother who was struggling to keep her daughter on her feet. "You'll feel better soon. You're not going to do this again, are you, sweetheart?"

The drive home was silent. Once back at the bus, the crowd had left. In the interim the boys had been fine with Jason, but now they just stopped and stared at the strained faces entering their home. No one was talking. No one was saying anything at all. Susan wondered what to do next. Glenn was relieved just to gather his wounded flock all together inside the metal fortress they called home. Once inside, Holly stumbled over and groped around for the ladder leading to her cubicle.

"Are you sure you want to go up there right now, Honey?" Her mother asked hesitantly. Susan didn't want her to disappear again, to remain hidden as she always did in her secluded cave, letting the thin closet paneling cut her off completely from the rest of the family.

"I just want to go to my room, Mom. That's all I want."

It took both parents to push her up the ladder and stuff her into her bed. The little door shut with a bang and no one in the bus said a word after that. They all stood around for awhile looking up to where Holly had disappeared. They all wondered what they could do.

One by one everyone found a spot somewhere in the bus and sat down quietly. The silence wore on as the night shadows quickly crept over and hid them in the stillness. Caleb and Kelly each crawled over and found someone's lap. Little whispers escaped Caleb's lips as his tiny green soldiers played imaginary wars in the arms of his big brother. They had quiet wars tonight. Jackie lay down burying herself in pillows. One by one, arms hugged one another, finding comfort. There were no candles lit tonight. Darkness protected them from the world, momentarily, while they sat in its peace. They listened for a long time just to hear the beautiful sound in their darkened home, a palpable relief they all were so thankful for. It was the sound of Holly being safe.

I am sending you out like sheep among wolves. Therefore be as shrewd as snakes and as innocent as doves.

Matthew 10:16 New International Version.

Seasons of Change

Summer days were sweet for the boys. Kelly had a young friend who lived on a boat nearby in a Marina Two slip. Daily, he begged to play with Crystal, and the three children could often be seen playing on the boardwalk of Marina Three. Two other little girls, Jennifer and Emily, occasionally joined the group, and they brought with them their pet duck, Lucky Ducky. Never tiring of the many things to explore at the busy harbor, they made do with the steel railings for a jungle gym and crawled over the rocks trying to catch tiny escaping crabs. Since Kelly and Caleb were not swimmers, their bulky orange life jackets were always strapped on whenever they stepped off the bus. Susan didn't care what it looked like or how much they protested. She simply knew better than to trust children, even knowing she would be right there watching them. The boys quickly adapted to new rules for new places and enjoyed themselves tremendously in the idyllic surroundings.

A new friend, Dianne, always had a bunch of teenagers and young adults hanging around her. They stood around the marina gate watching the children play.

"You should keep a close eye on your kids," warned Dianne. "Don't let your kids get near anyone's boat unsupervised and don't let them be separated from you. Some of these rich boat owners will say you are endangering their property, even if it is innocent. They don't care."

"I don't. I mean, I don't let them be unsupervised. At least I don't think I do." Susan answered.

"You should hold their hands even on the docks when you walk past the boats. I'm saying you have to be extra careful. I have raised these kids here on the harbor, and I have seen some terrible things. I have seen cops come out with guns drawn and boarded a boat just so they could take the kid. It was a single dad who truly loved his kid. You have to be very careful if you try to have kids here."

Susan thought probably more was involved in the story. Maybe it was drugs or something more criminal, but she kept her opinion to herself. This lady was hunkered down against the harbor patrol and she had her reasons.

"I had a bad experience already and we are being very careful. Thanks for the tip."

"I'm telling you..." Dianne continued. "If they can get you separated they can say you were endangering them. They will snatch them and that will be it!"

Susan just stared at her and the kids standing around her who were now all nodding their heads in agreement. They looked sad and serious. If this was true it would be unthinkable that in America...no, there must be more to this story. And so she had tucked it away in her mind to think about for later, but one sunny day later came.

Kelly and Crystal had disappeared from the spot they had permission to be in. Crystal's mother, Sharon, had been standing and talking with Susan and they hadn't looked over at the kids for a few minutes. It had been long enough. There wasn't a sign of them anywhere.

Susan frantically looked in every direction. "This is not possible. They can't be gone." Instantly, she conjured up images of children drowned or kidnapped and felt like running in all directions at once.

"Sharon!" she shouted as she started to run. "You look on that side, and I'll call the Harbor Patrol immediately to start a search. Then I'll cover the other side of the harbor where they might have wandered, okay?"

"Oh, no!" Sharon answered. She motioned for Susan to come back and in a guarded, quiet tone she spoke, "You must never call them. That would be the worst thing you could do."

Susan stared at Sharon like an alien from another planet. "What could be worse than a couple of drowned kids?" She asked sharply. "Can you tell me what? Does Crystal even swim?"

"Well, she does a little. But Susan," repeated Sharon with a strange, fearful look, "you must never call the Harbor Patrol. We have to do everything we possibly can and then still I wouldn't call them. It would be very bad."

Susan stared at her incredulously. She had come to know this woman as a highly concerned and responsible mother who was interested in every detail of her child's life, and now a completely different person seemed to be standing before her.

"Okay, Sharon." There was something about her look that was genuine fear, and of what she did not know, but seeing the caution was enough to make her decide to heed the warning. "Let's walk all around this harbor. I hope we'll find them playing and everything will be all right.

Sharon continued to talk in her quiet, soothing voice as the two women searched. Several times Susan wanted to give up and call for help, but fought her instincts as she tried to absorb the rules of this new world she had fallen into.

"I think I see them," Susan shouted. "There they are! Look over there!" She pointed, waving her hand and directing Sharon to look to the rocks below.

"Are you sure?" Sharon asked hopefully.

"Uh-huh. It's them. How did they ever get way over here?" she muttered to herself.

"Looks to me like they went digging for crabs and just kept finding them further and further away," said Sharon.

Both mothers pounced on the scalawags when they finally caught up to them and scolded them properly.

"Kelly! Don't you ever scare me like that again. Do you understand young man?" She pulled the startled boy up with her Vulcan neck pinch, grabbing him toward her.

"Oww! Sorry, Mom. Just looking for crabs and I...oww. I won't do it again, I promise. Owwiee! Sorry."

Crystal received a much quieter, gentle lecture about worrying her mother and nobody wanting anything bad to happen to her, and it wasn't nice to disobey. Crystal appeared equally sorry.

With great relief they all began their long trek back to the parking lot. As the children chattered happily about the critters that kept getting away from them, Susan thought back to the warnings given by Dianne and then remembered the events of this day and how frightened Sharon had been at just the mention of asking for help. What could have caused such a mysterious reaction from Sharon, Susan wondered? She decided to heed the voices of their wisdom and ignore the way she thought things should be, ignore how things had always been. She would proceed more cautiously in this new world where the sharks one should worry about weren't in the water below, but wore badges and lurked around corners of wood and stone to catch their prey, the tasty morsels of the poor and needy.

"My grace is all you need. My power works best in weakness." So now I am glad to boast about my weakness, so that the power of Christ can work through me. That's why I take pleasure in my weaknesses, and in the insults, hardships, persecutions, and troubles that I suffer for Christ. For when I am weak, then I am strong.

2 Corinthians 12:9-10 New Living Translation.

Front Page Introduction

Strolling through the parking lot, a short red-haired lady in white tennis shorts called out to Susan as she passed her sitting on the front steps of the open bus doors. "Have you heard of the new thing opening up for homeless children?"

Her round, wrinkled face was cheerful and encouraging as Susan looked up from holding the hair she was in the middle of French braiding for Jackie.

"It's brand new," she continued, "and it's for anyone who is homeless and has small children. I saw your little guys here," she pointed at Kelly and Caleb who were perched next to their mom, "and I thought I would mention it to you. Anyhow, it's supposed to be a place that's safe for kids to spend their days. They named it Storyteller or something like that, and it is right by the park where they have the downtown Head Start." The sweet lady kept moving and waved as she made her way to the boardwalk.

"I know where that's at," Susan replied.

Curiosity kept the little lady's remarks swirling inside Susan's head for the next few days, and finally she decided to drive over to the Head Start school. A tall, slender, middle-aged woman with an angular face was wearing a simple, green, calico dress and standing in the open doorway. Her long, straight, gray hair was tied neatly behind her.

"Hi, I'm Sarah." The strong European accent exuded lots of energy as the woman reached enthusiastically for Susan's hand. "Have you heard about our Storyteller? This place is going to be a refuge for children," she gushed excitedly.

"Yes. That's why I'm here," Susan answered, looking down at her boys beside her. "We are technically homeless, although I don't feel like I am. I almost feel guilty coming here because we think we have a nice home, but I guess we qualify. I would like to find out about your program." She waited, thinking about what to say next. She wasn't sure herself why she was here. "We live in a bus we keep parked in the harbor lot, and we have a boat in Free harbor. You see there is no legal place to park the bus so that's what makes us homeless." Susan watched the lady's face for a reaction.

She didn't hesitate. "Children will come here and escape whatever stresses they have to endure from not having a place to go." She smiled brightly, looking down at Kelly and Caleb. A refined lady who needed no makeup to showcase her attractiveness, Sarah was totally comfortable meeting children. "These are two, fine, young men." She leaned down and spoke directly to them with a voice matching her cheerful smile, "Boys, if you come here, we will find many fun and exciting things for you to do. You will learn lots of new things. Would you like that?"

Kelly nodded as he peeked inside and looked around the room filled with bright colorful displays and as many toys as would be found in a toy shop.

Caleb looked at his mother and pointed his finger at something just inside the door. "Hey, one of those is in my woom. Huh, Mom? Caywub has one of those."

"Oh yeah. I guess you do, Caleb," Susan answered distractedly, trying to take it all in with a glance.

Sarah's grace and charm was having a magical effect as Susan momentarily forgot she and her husband never left the boys with anyone. Without knowing why, Susan was in agreement with Sarah's idea that this might provide a temporary oasis. It felt like a safe place.

The two women talked about the program while watching the boys play. It was the first of its kind. It was evident Sarah had high expectations of her new venture. Many pieces of paper were filled out to allow the boys to stay for the next couple of hours, but Susan did not leave. She wanted them to get comfortable with where they were.

"We have to go now boys. Tell Miss Sarah goodbye." They ran to their mother's side and waved to their new teacher.

Sarah waved back. "Goodbye. You are going to be my first children, and I can't wait to see you again tomorrow. I have more signed up who will come, but you were my very first."

"Do we really get to play there every day, Mom?" Kelly asked. He was a jumping bean the rest of the day. He chattered with his brother about what he was going to do in the new place, and Susan was encouraged by the enthusiasm.

The next morning as Susan brought the boys to the day care center she noticed several people milling about and filling the small classroom. In the crowd were some who were taking pictures. A mother with her two children sat next to a cameraman, and she was giving him the spelling of their names. Sarah stood in the center of the room talking with a petite lady dressed in a black skirt and white tailored short-sleeved blouse. A little plastic ID badge was pinned to the woman's pocket, with easy to read words of News Press printed in bold type. She held a pen and pad close to her face, furiously scribbling on it.

Sarah nodded in Susan's direction as the family walked into the room. "This is Susan Dunn and this lady has quite a different homeless story." The reporter looked up and smiled.

"Yes." Susan smiled back at Sarah and the stranger as she stepped forward to shake the lady's hand. The hand was tiny with long, thin fingers, and Susan took note of her starched, white collar standing crisply at attention at the nape of her neck. "Nice to meet you. Well, I have a home and a boat but no land. I guess I'm considered homeless."

The attention of the reporter moved from Sarah and turned toward the three new arrivals. She asked several questions in the space of two minutes, and Susan did her best to share honestly what the family was enduring.

"Mrs. Dunn," the short-haired brunette began, "would you care if we do a story in the near future about your rather unusual situation? I have to check with my editor first, but I find this extremely interesting."

"Sure. I don't mind," Susan replied. "You can find us down at the harbor. We have the boat in a slip now because we're working on it."

"Thank you, and look for your boys' picture in the paper tomorrow. This daycare is a great idea, don't you think?" Her words conveyed a contagious enthusiasm as she turned away from Susan and resumed writing furiously on her pad, peppering Sarah with many questions.

The following day the cherubic faces of Kelly and Caleb stared up at anyone who glanced at a newsstand or opened their morning paper. Susan gasped when she saw it and grabbed the handle of the paper machine with shaking hands.

"How cute!" She pounced gleefully on the paper and

stood by the machine, staring at it in amazement. Rolling it up and hugging it close, she struggled to regain composure and stuff the quick display of joy in exchange for the safer non-emotional mask. Scanning the boardwalk, it was a relief to see few strollers out at this early hour. No one had seen her. She raced back through the parking lot, hurrying to show everyone at the bus. Shaking with excitement, she stumbled at the entrance and finished by crawling up the stairs.

"Maybe nobody will ever know it, but these are my boys!" she announced proudly, flashing the paper in the air with a grand flourish. Heads popped up and peered around from each of the cubbyholes to see what mom was showing.

Susan paused to catch her breath. "And if nothing ever happens again at least this one time the world got a chance to meet them! Oh, look!" she said, staring intently with her face close to the page. "They are just so cute!" She flashed the paper in their direction so they could see.

Turning to look at the two little rascals who had been rolling around on the floor she added, "and you are such good little boys too." They had stopped what they were doing, and now two sets of big, brown eyes stared at their mom. Nodding solemnly, they gave their mother what they hoped was the proper and serious response, and then both turned and went back to playing with their trucks.

Soon after on that same morning, the lady from the News Press along with a photographer arrived to do her story.

"Please come in. I am so happy to be able to welcome you into our home." Susan pulled the door handle and motioned for the couple to enter. "Let me introduce you to the rest of the family."

They both appeared excited to meet the family and

continued to look around while admiring the interior.

"Oh, my! Look at these skylights! I love this!" She glanced back at her partner who was nodding in agreement.

"This is fantastic!" he said.

"Come on back and have a seat so we can talk," Glenn offered. The cameraman chose to sit in the front, separating himself from the conversation, but they seated the reporter on a small rocking chair. It was near the rear of the bus and placed on a 4x6 red Persian rug. Susan sat on the swing at the rear door and Glenn perched on a folding chair.

"I just love how bright and cheery it is inside and..." she looked around at the cabin upper-half of the bus, "this wood is beautiful. You said it is cedar siding? It feels like home and it feels like Tom Sawyer-rustic with the bedroom lofts." Her eyes caught the words on a little wooden plaque hanging over the rear door. She whispered, "I am the way, the truth, and the life."

Caleb popped his head over the 1x12 keeping him safe in his upper room. "Hey, I got Lego's!" he announced, holding his big blocks up as a trophy. "Wanna see my Lego's?" He offered, leaning over the side and looking down at the new person sitting below.

"Look at him up there! He looks very content in his little space, and he certainly isn't going to fall with that big board holding him in."

"Nope. He's a regular little monkey. He crawls over into it every night after going to bed with us for a few minutes." Glenn chuckled. "He always asks us if we are tired yet, and when we say yes, it's his signal to crawl into his bed. Caleb is a real sweetheart."

The lady stared back and forth from the two locations where Glenn had been pointing. "He crawls over from that loft to his bed and never falls? I don't see how he manages."

"Of course I always shadow him, but no, he never has missed a step. I'm telling you he may only be three, but he is a little monkey."

"Well, I guess so." She shook her head admiringly. "So tell me how this all came about. I have lots of time and I'm not in any hurry." She returned to her little notebook and held the pencil up, ready. "Whatever gave you the idea to do this?"

Susan explained their whole story from beginning to end, at least the end they were presently experiencing. A considerable history had developed already with the saga of the boat, and nothing but a series of failures could be reported in the many attempts to get it operational.

"We put over a thousand dollars into getting the engine repaired, and then discovered to our dismay that the transmission also needed repairs." Susan continued, "We are working against time because in the immediate future winter storm conditions will cost us a tremendous amount of money towing this boat in and out of the harbor." Pulling a long strand of hair out of her face, she tucked it behind her ear and stared momentarily off into space.

"Plus," she said, her attention once again riveted upon the reporter, "the daily slip fees will be charged for berthing. It isn't always possible to arrange a tow. Wind and waves wait for no one.

Glenn interrupted, leaning forward, "We try not to, but we worry all the time about not being able to save our boat."

Susan nodded in agreement and then continued. "We do trust the Lord, but we still have to make the decisions, and if it sinks we will lose our link to legality. You see, that is also our link to hanging onto our kids." Susan paused for the full magnitude of the truth to sink in.

121

Realization caused the woman to slowly look up from her tablet. The pencil point stopped in the middle of the word she had been writing. She had been trying to get all of Susan's words. Now she got this mother's full meaning. She met Susan's desperate stare. No one spoke for a few moments.

Glenn broke the silence. "If it's never able to go on its own power, it's only a matter of time before we run out of money trying to save it or weather conditions catch us by surprise." He looked sadly down at his sandals, staring vacantly. He had searched for answers, but none were on the way. The couple clung to the shreds of their faith while they waited for some kind of deliverance.

The sweet lady looked thoughtful for a long time, as though pondering a solution to the dilemma herself. Quiet moments went by before she returned to her tablet and resumed writing. She kept shaking her head as though she should have an answer for the situation, but nothing would come.

The photographer had been patiently sitting at the front of the bus. Sensing the end of the interview when he saw his partner stand, he took his cue and called out, "I'd like to get a group shot of the whole family, and I'd really like to take this shot with everyone standing on the boat."

"I'm out of here. I'm not going to be in any paper," announced Holly, running in front of the startled man with the camera and causing him to take a step back. She jumped off the step and ran quickly in the direction of the phones at the Marina.

"No way! Not me either!" shouted Jackie, chasing after her sister. "Wait for me, Holly!" she yelled. "I'm going with you."

"Gee! I don't get that reaction very often." The man smoothed his balding hair, looking puzzled. "Most kids want to be in the paper," he chuckled as he peered through his lens and adjusted them for the light outside.

The photographer was escorted to where the boat was docked. Susan apologized to the man for the absence of the girls while he positioned the remaining family for the picture in the boat. She wanted to explain how the girls were feeling. Since she didn't understand their reactions herself, this was difficult.

"I think they are letting us know how mortified they are with having the whole town know of our plight. It has suddenly become obvious to me they don't like the exposure, and I imagine they can't take the embarrassment. I'm sorry about your picture, but even more sorry about what they showed us. I didn't know."

Glenn added, "We have been so busy trying to cope. I'm afraid we haven't been much help with the suffering of the girls or my son."

The photographer was kind and didn't seem concerned. He had his picture in a few moments. "I'm just going to go over and get one of the bus if you don't mind. I really like this bus."

They checked through the pages of each paper for a few days and were beginning to think maybe the editors had changed their mind about doing a story, but one morning while Susan was walking to the newsstand the faces of her family stared back at her from behind the little plastic cover of the machine. They were standing on their boat, along with the bus in all of its glory splashed across the Monday paper.

"Wow!" she whispered. "It is so big, taking up the whole page. Oh, my!" She never thought it would be made into a front page sensation, never realized what she would feel with this kind of promotion. Wanting to hide but forcing herself to walk calmly and quickly, she tried not to look at anyone while making her way back.

"Front page, guys," she announced quietly. "They plastered us all over the front page of the Monday paper."

Everyone jumped and ran to see, all trying to grab at once.

"Hold on. I will read it out loud. First, you can all see the picture," she said holding it up." Anxiety was crawling up her back as she contemplated what the words would say. She almost didn't want to know.

Jason peered down from his upper room. "I can see they did a good job of getting the bus and the boat. Glad I wasn't here."

"We were here, but we ran when we heard they were going to take pictures," Holly said. "I wasn't going to let them get me in that." She still seemed quite interested in spite of her words. "That's a good picture of you, Mom. Kelly isn't smiling."

"Let me see," Kelly grabbed the paper from below. "Hey, how come I'm not smiling? I was sure I smiled."

"You look fine, Kelly. Don't worry."

Kelly reassured, shrugged. Then he looked at his mom and said, "We are in the paper again, Mom. That's a lot of times, huh?"

"Oh yeah. That's a lot." She nodded with uplifted eyebrows and then began to read the article, stopping frequently as everyone had lots to say about what was written.

"It says here they don't want my kids hanging out at the

harbor." Susan looked up at the eyes all staring in her direction. "Well, what about other people's kids? I guess they are okay."

"What?" Jackie peered over her mother's shoulder. "Where?"

"Right here...and it says they don't want to be a social worker for me. Well, looky there. I don't want them for one either."

"They don't even want us walking around in the harbor, Mom?" The words had pierced Holly.

"Oh, wow!" Susan quit reading.

"What, Mom? What does it say?" Jason's jaw tightened, bracing himself for what might come.

"It says they want to make an ordinance banning any vehicle taking up two spaces."

"They want to get rid of us that bad?" He shook his head.

"They called us unsightly, and they are worried about the welfare of the children...said we are an eyesore."

It was lengthy and the interruptions frequent, but finally they got through it.

"Just want to hide forever," Susan announced. "That nice reporter did a good job with our side of things, but I am mad about what the harbor patrol said about us. Their words are crushing. Where does their prejudice come from? They don't even know us, and they don't want to either. I feel I have to do something."

"Now you know how we feel, Mom," Holly said.

"Oh honey, this is so hard. I'm not going to let this go. This feels like we have been thrown into the middle of some kind of a war, a war against kids and the parents who love them. We aren't anybody important—just parents who love each other and who only want to go to work and stay a family.

They are making it out like we are some kind of disease or enemy of the state. I just read what everybody else thinks about us, and now the whole world needs to hear what I think. It's time I wrote a letter to the editor."

Behold, they shall surely gather together, but not by me; whosoever shall gather together against thee shall fall for thy sake...No weapon that is formed against thee shall prosper; and every tongue that shall rise against thee in judgment thou shalt condemn. This is the heritage of the servants of the Lord, and their righteousness is of me, saith the Lord.

Isaiah 54:16-17 King James Version Holy Bible

Cornered

Scribbling furiously, the words poured out as Susan's hand dug into the school-lined paper, scratching out parts of lines as she reworked thoughts.

"...I think it is important to realize that when we moved into our bus-cabin, I didn't suddenly become an unfit mother, regress into criminal behavior, obtain moronic unintelligence, or lose my job skills.

We do not look to the government to help us, only to decriminalize us. We look to the Lord daily because we are well aware of how needy we are, but had he not been leading us we would never have survived thus far. Many people have voiced concern over the safety of our children. Be assured I share those concerns, even to a greater degree, but I believe the same God who delivers one person from cancer and another from catching AIDS is the same God that I have to trust to keep our boat from sinking. I also believe he expects mothers to keep a good eye on their children; so the harbor patrol can relax as I won't be requiring their assistance as my social worker..."

Susan spent several more paragraphs bragging about how wonderful each of her kids were. She wrote of her determination to put motherhood and family first and how proud she was of her grown kids. Finally, she finished off by saying

"...Santa Barbara may think we are homeless but I don't happen to share that opinion. If the home I've built for my family is an eyesore, then perhaps it would be better to look away. We have nothing on this earth to share but ourselves, and of that we will never be ashamed. My existence is not qualified by what I own but rather who I am. I invite you to discover who that person is."

Reworking the letter, she continued until she felt it was perfect. The margins were filled with scribbled in changes. "There!" she said finally. "Now I need about five minutes to type this up."

No one heard. The boys were in Storyteller, and everyone else had left for various reasons. She needed to be alone to think, alone to process the anger and also to get the courage to say the words. She slowly read the letter the editor would receive.

"Boy, I'm really telling them off, Lord." She stared at the strong words, reading them carefully again and again. "But I don't care! They are wrong and they need to hear this. I am telling the whole world, and I don't care what anyone thinks about it!"

She wondered if the Lord felt as strongly about this as she did. She certainly hoped so. A finished version was quickly typed, and the short journey to the News Press office begun. Susan felt an almost frantic need to get this to them immediately but didn't know why. Maybe she would lose her courage to do it.

"Lord, I'm asking you," she prayed, "please let this get printed and I will just try to calm down."

Praying while she walked, she never noticed the beautiful, pink, flowering bushes along the sidewalk. "I need to get over this but I also need to be able to defend us, and I think this is the best way. Jesus, I hope you agree," ...never noticed the hordes of chattering tourists walking by on their way to the shops and beaches.

"They're picking on innocent kids. They have to know that, and they don't care"...and never noticed the people sitting outside at the sidewalk cafe enjoying their coffees and sweets.

"Please, please help me do something." Fear and apprehension clung like a muggy jacket, growing in intensity as she grew closer to the imposing structure of the big building in De La Guerra Square. Clutching the typed letter in one hand, she looked up and paused briefly to stare at the News Press sign.

Susan took a deep breath. "Okay, so I'm at the door, and I'm really doing this, God. Help me. Just help me," she continued to pray quietly while forcing one foot to go in front of the other. People, if they even heard, paid no attention. They were busy, busy, busy with their important business.

"Oh yeah...in Jesus name, amen."

Once inside, the busy crowds swallowed her up and carried her along in their midst. It had been easy to find the right place, easy to drop the letter off, and easy to walk back outside. Fear gave up and left her alone for the time being, and Susan took deep gulps of air standing once again in the beautiful park.

"Okay. That's all I can do," she announced. A strange new excitement accompanied her on her walk. Peace was restored. "Beautiful flowers," remarked Susan.

At the harbor a parade of cars circled the lot, all wanting to see the bus they had been introduced to that morning on their front page.

"This has been going on since you left. Nothing like before, Mom," Jackie reported. This is so exciting. Scary, really. What is going to happen? Do you think they are friendly?"

"Have no idea. I think we are going to find out, though," her mother answered.

Many residents of the harbor came to the family expressing unhappiness with the news story. They were outraged at the prejudice and mean spirit coming from the harbor patrol. They hadn't known.

A pleasant older woman in a gray suit drove up in a late-model Mercedes. Leaving it running, she hopped out and handed a large bag to Susan. "Here's a sleeping bag you can have. It was my son's. I read the story in the paper. Oh, and here's some money to buy another. Bye now. I wish I could do more." After depositing her gifts, she left as quickly as she came.

"Thank you so much! I appreciate this!" Susan called after her and waved. "We really need it. Thank you."

A strolling, elderly couple walking hand-in-hand called out as they walked around the bus. "Oh, I wish we were younger and we could do something like this. We always admire it when we walk by. It certainly is not an eyesore!"

At about the same time, a young lady marched up, holding a brightly colored red and white ice chest.

"Hi. My name is Nancy. I brought you an ice-chest we don't need anymore. I read that you need one."

"Yes," answered Susan gratefully. "I really do. Won't you come in? I would love to get to know you."

The red and white ice chest came in with the beautiful young lady, and Susan sat down with her to get acquainted. A knock on the glass door interrupted them. "Oh, it's the reporter. Excuse me just a moment, please."

She reached over and grabbed the bar to open the doors. "Hi, there! Thank you for the story. It was much bigger than

I was expecting."

"I just stopped by for a moment to give you this. Someone donated money for a sleeping bag, and I thought I would bring it. I can't stay. I have to go, but here. Take this."

"This is great. We will use this. Thank you very much."

Susan returned to her guest. While visiting, she was happy to learn her new friend also loved the Lord and went to the local Catholic church. Staring at the ice chest and listening to Nancy, Susan became increasingly aware of uncomfortable feelings. Her stomach churned with anxiety as the confusion engulfed her. Apparently, receiving gifts was difficult. She was extremely grateful for the cash gift, however, and was reminded again how the Lord provides in mysterious ways.

No one outside of the family was aware of a desperate need they had. A few days earlier they had been given a prescription for Caleb they couldn't fill. He had been sick and they had taken him to the free clinic where it was determined he needed antibiotics for an infection, but the clinic didn't dispense free medications. The money she had been given would just cover the $38.00 cost of his penicillin. They had been afraid to tell anyone for fear they would be judged as bad parents, and decided to wait for the next paycheck to start the medicine. Holding the bills tightly in her hand, she now knew her little boy would be all right.

Immediately twinges of guilt hit her as the money had been given for a needed sleeping bag, but she knew it was more important for Caleb to get the medicine and she hoped no one would find out. Surely they would forgive her, but there was so much uncertainty now, no one to confide in or trust. Oh Lord, she prayed silently. Why do I even have to feel bad for something like this? This is nuts.

That night the tired couple laid under the rosy-hued streetlight directly overhead listening to the quiet breathing of Caleb next to them. The greater part of their bedroom roof was a large triangle of Plexiglas. It made one feel as though the sky could be touched and the stars were directly in front like a huge TV screen. They could see satellites moving across the atmosphere and planes were clearly visible by their running lights as they passed over on their way to Goleta airport. It was a favorite part of life in the bus, and each little sleeping area had its own skylight. Lying still, they heard a man with his wife talking while passing underneath their window. Sound traveled perfectly through the metal walls, and anything ever said was easily heard.

"Don't worry, honey. It won't be here much longer. We have it all taken care of."

"Well, I sure hope so," a female voice answered. "You really think the ordinance will work?"

"I know it will," the man answered.

Susan looked at her husband, perplexed. He shrugged his shoulders.

"No idea," he whispered.

The poor are shunned by all their relatives—how much more do their friends avoid them! Though the poor pursue them with pleading, they are nowhere to be found.

Proverbs 19:7 New International Version.

The Visitors

"Mom! Someone's here." Kelly looked sheepishly at the visitors, staring through the glass.

It was early the next day and the boys were excited about going to the pool. The bus was parked a few feet away, and the baby pool was open and free to the community during the summer months. They were packing their bags and getting a snack ready to go. This was not just for fun but it was presently their bathing method, and Susan would sit discreetly in the water with them.

"Hello! Mrs. Dunn?" A smiling and friendly appearing middle-aged woman in a beige, silk blouse and brown skirt stood next to an older fellow with a balding ring of white hair and wearing a dark-brown suit. They both wore glasses, big smiles, and held briefcases.

Oh, no! Jehovah Witnesses, Susan thought. Right when we are leaving. She reached over and pulled the bar so the doors opened wide.

"Good morning. Uh...we were just leaving..."

"Oh, this won't take long. I am Virginia Scott and I am from Child Protective Services," she announced cheerfully, very cheerfully.

Susan must have turned a different color because she quickly added, "I just want you to know that being homeless is not against the law, and you are not breaking any laws for what you are doing. We have been called to come and pay a visit, and so we would like to offer you all of the services that can assist you if you ever want. We are not saying you need services, but it would be good to know where they are if you do."

The man quickly nodded his head like a puppet, smiling back and forth at Susan and Virginia Scott. "Yes, that could be helpful if you ever do."

"We don't like to have to come to some of these calls, but we are required by law to do so when someone calls us. That is the only reason we are here."

"Yes, the only reason," the man in the brown suit parroted, continuing to nod and looking very convincing. "I really like this bus."

"Mommy, we go to pool now?" Caleb interrupted, tugging at his mother's shorts.

"Real soon, Cabey." She reached down and pulled him close to her for a leg hug, patting his head. "Real soon. Be patient."

"This is great," the man gushed. You can get to the pool anytime from here, and you have done a remarkable thing with this bus, just remarkable."

Clearly, the couple felt uncomfortable, and from their huge smiles and strained faces they were emphatically attempting to convey they meant no harm. Susan wasn't convinced, but she did begin to relax from their friendly show of support.

"I bet they like the pool," Virginia said, looking down at the two boys.

"They love it. We go every day. Won't you come in? We have plenty of time later for the pool. I just thought you were Jehovah Witnesses."

"Oh, no. We don't need to come in. We don't want to stay. We just want to give you these papers that show you all the places you can go. You may already know this stuff, but we are here to help. Child Protective Service supports families and our goal is to help any way we can." She handed a pack of papers to Susan.

As Susan reached down to take the papers she heard the back door slam and instantly knew what had just happened. "Excuse me," she hollered, racing for the back. She shoved the door open and hopped out, snagging the scalawag by the arm before he could get two parking spaces away. She held tightly to his chubby little arm.

"Oh no, you don't. Do not leave without Mommy!" she scolded while marching him back to where the couple was standing. "Do you understand me, mister?"

"You said we going to the pool. I just going to the pool, Mommy." Caleb, looking frustrated and confused, stared at his mom.

Susan acknowledged her very surprised visitors. "I knew when I heard the door slam that he was making an escape. Can't trust him for a moment, and I had already unlocked the back door because we were about to leave. We always go out the back door," she said while grasping tightly to his hand. "I apologize for that."

"Oh, no. Don't you worry about a thing. We know how kids are, and you were right on top of things."

"You sure were," the man echoed, still smiling and shaking his head admiringly.

"We won't keep you anymore, Caleb. I just want you to know, Mrs. Dunn, that you can call me anytime and for anything. I mean that. Here is my card. Keep it handy. Everyone doesn't feel the way we do, and you may need a friend sometime." Her smile dropped momentarily, and she glanced disapprovingly in the general direction of the marina. "It has been nice to make your acquaintance. You boys have fun now, okay?"

They turned and left, and for some reason Susan felt better than she had in weeks. The worst had happened, the dreaded CPS visit. Instead of feeling afraid, she felt like she might have allies. Strange but it seemed as if feared enemies were changing places with perceived friends. The world was turning upside down, and even after Caleb did the worst by giving them something to write her up for, she still felt they could be trusted. Wow, getting paranoid sure makes you feel desperate, Susan thought. CPS as friends was a novel concept that had not proved to be true for others she knew.

At the pool, Susan glanced through the stack of papers. There was information she knew about, but a few things were new. She tossed them into her backpack, then slid into the water with the splashing boys. Filled with shame and embarrassment, she imagined everyone was staring. They probably all know I am trying to sneak a bath. Pushing that to the back of her mind, she began to play with Caleb. His favorite game was shark.

"I'm going to get you. Here I come," she said, blowing bubbles and making dun, dun, dun, dun noises. "It's the big sharky."

"No, Mommy, no!" Caleb squealed and giggled, splashing and running from his mom.

"Who else can I eat?" She crawled on her elbows and spun around to come after Kelly, rolling in the water.

"Whoa. I better get outta Dodge," he hollered and started running across the pool. She laughed and sat up in the few inches of water. Apparently there were more children who wanted to play shark too. Several joined in with splashing and squeals. Some of the moms didn't want their babies around so much commotion, and began taking them aside.

"No, guys," Susan interrupted. "We have to be careful of the babies. No more sharky. Sorry." She got out of the water and sat on the grass, looking at the many young moms gathered for this fun event. Making friends came easily to her and with whoever was around, but now she didn't want that to happen. Before, there had never been a stranger. Now, things were different. She didn't know why and she didn't know how, but they were.

Susan listened to snippets of conversation in the air and pretended nothing had changed, that she was still a part of the life she had always known. She pretended they were her friends and it was a regular day at a beautiful park. All the children were playing together and she was a normal American mother. Nobody here knew she lived in the bus parked a few feet away and that she was able to keep her kids only because she owned a boat parked in the ocean. I still look pretty normal, she thought. I could be a tourist. They don't live here either. If you don't belong anywhere then where does it matter where you choose not to belong? She chuckled at the thought. Her status gave her a lifetime perspective others didn't know. She looked around at the beautiful scenery as if she had every right to be there.

"Boys, it's time to go home." Gathering up the backpack, Susan handed out towels to the dripping boys and they slowly made their way across the parking lot. "You know, guys, I was born in this town. My mom had her picture taken right over there on that boardwalk." Susan pointed over a few yards from where they were walking. "That means she walked these same streets that we walk, and she probably did the same things we are doing."

"I didn't know that, Mom." Kelly looked at his mother. "Where is she now?"

"She got sick and died, but I remember her. I was a

toddler, but I still remember. I also remember places in town like the City Market. We used to go there in an old, black, 1939 coupe. That is, we went whenever my mom could get it to start. I only know that because when I got older I recognized the same car in several old movies. It was a popular model.

My cousins and I would get jammed in the back of that little car. It didn't actually have a seat in the back. There were no seat belts or car seats in those days, and we would jump up and down while the car was moving. I remember getting squished. I think I was the younger cousin. After my brother was born, I got put on a pink leash which I thought was great fun.

I remember playing on the railroad tracks behind Summerland Fire Station when my mom was in the hospital for so long. My dad worked at the fire station and sometimes they would take me to see him. I never saw him out of his uniform, and he smelled funny. I figured out later it was cigar smoke and probably sweat. I don't think he used much deodorant. Strange what kids remember.

They gave me away before my mom died, but I got to see her one last time. I know I still have relatives all over this area, but I don't know who any of them are. I never belonged to anyone or any place after that, but I belong to this town. So, that is probably why we are here now." She looked down at her two boys intently taking in every word.

"I feel like I belong on every street we drive on," she said, turning and looking toward State Street. "God sent me here for some reason, and I intend to find out what it is."

When thou passest through the waters, I will be with thee; and through the rivers, they shall not overflow thee: when thou walkest through the fire, thou shalt not be burned; neither shall the flame kindle upon thee.

Isaiah 43:2 King James Version

Fire

Beautiful days came and went as always in the Mediterranean playground. Tourists walked the perfect streets oowing and aawing at everything provided for them to sample and enjoy. At the same time, the Dunns were experiencing an equal environment but with a different perspective from their corner of paradise.

The city had prevailed in their ticket against the Dunns, teaching the family the judicial department had no reason to defend them or their rights. Directly following this lesson, a special ordinance had been presented to and later passed at City Council which banned all vehicles taking up two spaces in the harbor lot. It was done to rid the harbor of the bus and them. Their crimes against society were they were disabled, had kids, and were poor. This ordinance stipulated a grandfather clause exclusively for their bus, extending a year in the harbor, but the family knew being seen in the harbor using this "special permission" would only incur more hatred. If others could no longer be in the lot, then they would refuse it also.

The next home would be Stearns Wharf parking lot, which they would refer to as One Santa Barbara. This place was away from most of the traffic and made it easier to hide. Everyone in the family wanted nothing more than to be left completely alone. Going to the harbor for any reason was a dreaded trip and so they watched their boat gently bob on the waves in front of them while sitting in their bus parked at the pier. They rarely went out to it and almost never brought it in.

Glenn stayed gone most of the time and Susan never knew where. He seemed lost to himself and to his family. The older kids wanted to stay anywhere except with their parents. The only interest the community had toward this family was in making them leave. Their church did not approve, and there was no family, friends, or community support of any kind. Extremely unwanted, everyone made sure that was understood. The Dunns, while daily chatting with and making tourists smile by taking their pictures next to the home they were so thankful for, had become the official pariahs of Santa Barbara.

Nevertheless, paradise was to be appreciated for all of its beauty. The afternoon shadows danced in the ocean breezes flitting through the palms of the parking lot. There was always something to be thankful for, and living in the atmosphere of love, peace, and joy was Susan's greatest aspiration. Every moment this could be grasped always caused her to praise the Lord. Glancing at the sailboats bobbing like corks, she felt the peace and safety that living on the edge of the world brought her.

"No matter where....we go...we are always at home," came the sound of a male voice from behind her back door. "We never leave HOME ...without it." Sounds of chuckling could be heard. The voice continued, "All of our home schooled kids are organically homegrown...If I were a carpenter— we'd have better furniture. But then again, if I were a carpenter I would probably have built us a house."

"Honey, get this one. This is good...When we leave, we always say—well, there goes the neighborhood." A female voice joined with the man in more laughter.

"Oh hey, what about this? We better get out of here before

Mr. Rogers finds out who the people are in his neighborhood...That's really good." More laughter.

Susan delighted in the constant stream of tourists who took pictures of her taped-on, homemade, bumper stickers she had at both ends of the bus. She loved making people laugh, and apparently the little sayings she thought of did just that. They sold a lot of Kodak film anyway. It always made her smile knowing people didn't realize there was a family inside listening to their joy.

"Did you see this?" The woman had moved to the front of the bus. She laughed loudly as she read, "They are still coming in covered wagons."

"Yeah, I already got all of those. Wait 'til you see the other side."

The lady continuing to read out loud said, "Yes, this is still a school bus because I'm doing my homework...Most photographed house in town...Motherhood is the small business of our future...If you think your kids are bouncing off the walls, you should see these boys swinging from the rafters....Honey," she paused momentarily, "do you think they have rafters?"

She looked up through the front window and caught a kind lady smiling back at her from inside. Susan waved a friendly greeting and pointed to the rafters. Embarrassed, the woman mouthed the word "sorry", ducked down and quickly moved from sight. The sounds of a car driving away could be heard. Often this was the time when one member of the Dunns would invite the strangers inside. They considered it an honor to entertain visitors from faraway places, and their guests were treated as royalty. Thoroughly welcomed, they would always leave with big smiles.

Susan looked down at the boys playing with their Lego's

and planes. They made happy little boy noises, completely unconcerned about the politics of life surrounding them. Jackie was sound asleep in the rear of the bus and Holly, as usual, was locked in her little room. Susan felt thankful they still had each other, whatever that meant, and she thought she had better get dinner started soon.

Standing at the stove, she carefully poured gasoline into the funnel. After setting the can down, she wiped out and put the funnel away, then started to pump up the stove before lighting it. It had become a familiar routine, and the dilapidated old stove with two of the three burners working served the family well. She never would know what exactly went wrong, but it seemed that right after igniting the fuel rod became separated from the burner. Either raw fuel or something in the bottom of the stove exploded into a huge ball of flame, instantly climbing the paper-thin, wooden, wall of the bus.

"Holly! Holly!" she screamed. "Get the boys and get out! Fire! Come on, Hurry!" She glanced behind looking for something to smother the flame. In an instant, the decision was made which of two blankets would be sacrificed while at the same time she kept trying to pull out the gas chamber she knew would explode at any moment.

"Jackie!" she shouted. "Wake up! Fire! Wake up, Jackie, and get out of here! Holly! Hurry up before this blows!"

Her frantic attacks of hitting the blanket against the walls were to her amazement, successful, but throwing the blanket on top of the stove and trying to smother the flames wasn't working at all. The flames were everywhere around her face and arms, and crazy thoughts raced through her mind. What's a few burns? I've got to try to save our home. It doesn't hurt yet. Staring at the flames all over her, she wondered why doesn't it hurt yet?

Horrified, she cried out, "This thing can't blow up before I get the kids out! Oh God, get the kids out before it blows!"

Holly moving in slow motion seemed more interested in watching her mother try to rip the stove away from the cords that held it fastened securely against the wall.

"Holly! Hurry up! This thing is going to explode any second!" In a panic, Susan tore at the strings, gouging her hands and arms while pulling with all of her might. Something was feeding the fire, and flames were shooting out underneath. Her efforts to smother it were futile. The flames licked at her clothes, the kitchen pots and dishes, food on the counter. She grabbed another blanket and tried to smother with that one, but in vain. Why, it's still not spreading, she thought. The fire should be spreading by now. My clothes should be catching. Lord, what is happening?

"Jackie, wake up!" she hollered one more time at the soundly sleeping girl less than a yard away.

"Oh, Mom," Holly said. "Don't get so excited." Slowly, ever so slowly she led the boys to the open door.

Just then, the last cord broke, and Susan grabbed the burning hot, flaming stove, carrying it outside and nearly having to push the kids out of the way. Shouting furiously at the top of her lungs, she yelled, "Holly, it is okay to get upset when it is a real emergency! This is going to blow at any moment, your sister is not going to wake up at all, the bus could burn down, and I can't get you to move!"

She was standing right behind her daughter, and this time when she yelled for Holly to get her the water jug the kid jumped for it. Quickly, the water doused the blackened blanket mess, the gas nozzle now turned off finally lost its fuel, and whatever had been burning on the bottom was drowned in steam and ashes. Susan raced back into the bus convinced she would find something burning. Miraculously nothing was.

"Jackie!" she yelled. "Wake up! There was a fire and you could have died, and you didn't even wake up!"

"Huh? What?" a sleepy voice rasped. But she didn't wake up.

Susan turned her attention on herself to see what kind of burns she was going to have to take care of, but except for the cuts and a few spots on her fingers where she carried out the hot stove nothing more could be seen. But Lord, she wondered as she continued to look for some sign of damage to her clothes, there were flames all over me. How could this be?

She glanced at the wall above where the stove had been and black streaks of smoke were everywhere, but she could feel no hot spots. She looked in the mirror expecting her eyebrows to be burned off or something, anything...no. Untouched!

Running out to the parking lot, she quickly scooped up the dying embers and put them into a metal can.

"Praise God!" she exclaimed. "They didn't see it. Praise God! There wasn't even enough smoke to get their attention. I'm so glad. I would rather have this bus burn up then get rescued by them," she rambled on, pacing back and forth.

The kids looked dumbfounded. This was a lot of excitement coming from a mother who never yelled.

"Woo hoo! I can't believe this turned out so well. Look, Holly." She turned to her and held out her arms. "I'm not burned anywhere. Not really. And you saw—you saw there were flames all over me. I should be burned. My clothes should be burned, but they aren't. I'm glad you are all okay.

I'm glad the bus is not burnt. Mostly I'm glad they didn't even know this happened. Hallelujah!" she shouted. "I'd die first before I would want to be rescued by the Harbor Patrol."

Confused, she thought back to the nice young men who had been so friendly. They had been there for the family when they needed help. That was another time, but they were the way she wanted to think of them, rescuers, keepers of law and order. She would have been proud if one of her sons grew up to be like them. One nation under God and justice for all...no, wait. That was a school memory. Not real. The police had always been her heroes, and now she was repulsed by the thought of having to see one. She wanted them to go back to being her heroes. It was all so upsetting.

Another memory surfaced as she paced back and forth in front of the bus. It was the walk in the harbor while looking for the lost kids, and she thought back to how surreal everyone acted when the Harbor Patrol was mentioned, even referring to them as Hitler. Life had changed dramatically since that day. Her whole world had gone through a radical transformation, and now the metamorphosis was complete. What Sharon felt, what Diane and the others felt—it was a part of her.

This isn't the neighborhood bully mocking me—I could take that.

This isn't a foreign devil spitting invective—I could tune that out.

It's you! We grew up together! You! My best friend! Those long

hours of leisure as we walked arm in arm, God a third party to our

conversation.

Psalms 55:12-14 The Message

Designated Driver

"The boys are at Storyteller and I have to go get some paperwork done for ..." Susan stopped mid-sentence as she caught sight of Glenn pacing at the back of the bus. She had just hopped out of the car and jumped onto the stairs, glad to see him inside and know he was finally home. She had news, but Glenn's appearance shocked her out of her thoughts. He looked terrible. He was white, shaky, and dripping wet. His shirt was soaked with sweat, and his eyes had a wild look to them.

"What's the matter?" she asked. "What happened to you?"

"Suzi," he croaked in a voice that was barely a whisper. "I have something I have to tell you."

"What happened to your voice? What is going on?" She was shaking her head with a terrible foreboding, but no clue what it could be. "You are dripping wet. Are you injured?"

He grabbed a towel lying beside him and began rubbing his face and neck. "Suzi," he cried like a plaintive little child. "I have to tell you something, honey. It's real bad. You were going to find out right away, and I wanted to tell you. I really did. Lots of times I wanted to tell you, but now you are going to find out when you check the bank account."

"The bank account?" Susan was totally confused.

"The money is all gone. I spent all the money, hon. I'm so sorry."

"What are you talking about? Why do you look this way? Your mouth is all funny when you talk, and you look terrible. Why are you sweating so much?" She watched water run off his face as he tried to mop it up. "Spent the money on what?"

The morning that had been so bright and full of promise suddenly seemed gray, and fear surrounded her as terrible news had just arrived, but she couldn't imagine what it was.

"I don't understand. What are you telling me?"

Glenn paced back and forth trying to get his courage up. He put the towel down, then immediately picked it up again and started wiping himself all over. "I'm a drug addict, honey. I'm a rotten drug addict. I mainlined cocaine," he said, holding his arm out for her to see as if she would know what that should look like. "I said I mainlined cocaine...and spent all the money on it. I did wrong, Suzi. I am so sorry. I don't know how you could ever forgive me."

"What are you saying?" She kept shaking her head, refusing to believe her best friend, her lover, her whole world for many years had just spoken these words, let alone actually did them. "What do you mean?"

"I mean I am a drug addict. I started on marijuana when we first came to the harbor, but the kids never told you. They didn't want you to know. I didn't want you to know. I tried to stop, honey. I really did. But then things got so bad and I don't know what happened. I got so upset when they were mean to us. I couldn't take it. I just couldn't take it."

"Since we came to the harbor?" she spoke almost in a whisper. "Things got bad for all of us. They are still bad." She stared at him. "Now they are worse it seems."

"I know, but I don't know what to do. I can't stop. The money is gone."

Susan kept thinking how strange his voice sounded. It wasn't him. He must still be on the drugs, she thought. He didn't look like her husband. She kept staring at the odd way his mouth kept moving and the way he had to keep wiping the sweat off.

"The kids knew?" she asked incredulously. What kids?" The horror was growing by the moment as his words finally sunk in. Had she heard right?

"Not the little boys," he tried to reassure, "but all the others. They knew. Holly came in one day while I was shooting up, and I made her hold the tourniquet while I did it. I told her this is what you never want to do, McHooley. Yep, I told her never to do it."

"What?" Susan's eyes flashed angrily at the man pacing back and forth in front of her, unable to sit for more than a moment. Where is my Glenn, she thought? What have you done with him? The one she had loved more than any other, and now?

"What? What are you saying?" Do you know what that would do to a young girl who loved and trusted her daddy? The same daddy who preached to her against using any drugs, or alcohol, even against listening to worldly music? I can't believe you are saying any of this. I can't believe any of this is happening."

"It's true, Suzi. It's all true." Glenn hung his head in shame.

"We were missionaries on the other side of the world. We served the same Jesus together and....and...do you even know what you did to Holly? "

He didn't. He was lost in his own private hell. Completely alone.

"That's not all," Glenn announced. He sat down under the glaringly bright light from overhead. "There's something worse than that."

"Glenn," she said firmly. "Do you know what you have

done? How could it be worse?"

He stared straight ahead at his wife and said with a shaking voice, "I used a dirty needle. I shared a needle with a bunch of drug addicts. I could have gotten AIDS and if I did, I already gave it to you."

Great! That's just great, she thought. She stared back at him shaking her head. She waited a few moments deciding if she should speak to him at all.

"So, we both die and the state raises the little ones. No one ever wanted me and no one will want them. We have already learned that now haven't we? CPS will take the boys as soon as they find out, you know. I mean these are the rules. We know the rules. They take kids when the parents don't do drugs. What do you think is going to happen to our innocent kids when their precious daddy gets them taken away to a scary place neither you nor I ever wanted for them?"

"I know, honey. I know. I am so sorry."

"You threw us away, Glenn. You threw us all away. I don't have a choice of what I can do. You threw me away, and I have to accept it. Thanks for everything, but now I only get the memories. Whether I have AIDS or not, I have to try to rescue the kids, try to find a way to keep them as long as I can. I don't want them feeling bad things about you. You have been their whole world. You have been everything to me too. I can get over it. I'm used to losing, but I will do everything in my power to protect them as long as I can. I don't want them to know everything you've done.

"I will do anything," Glenn cried. "I can't lose my family. I will go into a program. Give me another chance." Glenn was crying and sweating. Snot was running down his face and shirt.

"You do that. You go in a program."

"I promise you, Suzi, I will get clean. I'll go to the mission right now and get in their program. I can do this. You'll see. I will leave right now. I have to do this for my boys, for you, honey."

"Do it for yourself. Somehow I have to deal with what you have done. You've made it so we can't be together. I love you, but I also love the little guys we brought into this world. They didn't choose to take drugs, and I didn't choose to raise them up alone on the streets, but now I have to."

Glenn stepped out of the bus and began walking. "You'll see. I can do this. I have to do this. I love you."

She watched him slowly disappear down the street getting smaller and smaller. She sat in the shadow of the open door on the bus steps for a long time, not feeling, not thinking. Her mind felt pleasantly numb. Jason found his mom still sitting there when he came home much later.

"Dad told me about the drugs," she said simply. "He's gone. Supposedly he's gone into the mission program. Now," she turned looking behind her at the driver's seat, "I have to learn to drive this."

His face showed no expression. "We knew, Mom." His voice was flat and monotone. "We didn't know what to do." Jason had been carrying a heavy load for a long time.

"There was nothing you could do, Jason. Nothing at all. This should never have happened."

Susan knew the time had come for her to drive the beast. The thought filled her with dread. "Right now I should pick up the boys, and then we get to watch me learn how to drive this."

"Let's drive it now before you get the boys, and I will help. You are going to need my arms if you have to turn left.

Remember? You can't turn the wheel if it is stopped. Too much weight overhead," he said pointing to the roof overhang in the front.

"Oh, I forgot about that. Yikes! This is so hard." Susan started to cry remembering yet another hindrance to her driving.

"We can do it, Mom. Don't worry."

They got the bus started easily enough, and Susan put it in granny gear to make sure it would go slow. She practiced by circling the lot a few times, and then she pointed herself in the direction of the narrow road leading out of the unmanned kiosk. She felt like a bull in an empty stadium with her son as the matador standing there waving his arms for her to go forward. She aimed the best she could, but one tire still climbed the curb.

"At least I didn't take out the kiosk building," she announced after safely getting onto the road.

Jason ran and jumped back on through the open doors of the slow moving vehicle. He yelled, "Good job! Don't stop now."

She put it in a higher gear, and the bus suddenly lurched forward jumping over the railroad tracks. "Not exactly the way to do that," she said as she heard things falling off of shelves behind her.

"Don't worry about that stuff. Keep going. You are doing fine." His encouragement was desperately needed.

Just over the tracks was the little dirt road they normally parked on at night. She made a rolling left turn and pulled right up into their spot, breaks squealing in protest even with the low speed.

"Did it!" It was a major victory. She turned the key off, but left it in and just sat there shivering in the warm afternoon.

Later that night, the doors were shut, the lights turned out, and a great sadness crawled in under the doors and in through the cracks of the little house on the asphalt prairie. Susan sat alone in the dark at the driver's seat holding the huge steering wheel and fingering the knobs of the Allison transmission beside her knee. She sat at the wheel for many hours staring out the window. The headlights of several cars flashed in her face as they drove by, and the bright streetlight streaming down over her head showcased Susan like an eerie non-moving statue one wouldn't expect to see. Thoughts going through her head were much the same as another had felt many long years ago. Their pain had been the same.

"But I cry to you for help, O Lord; ....Why, O Lord, do you reject me and hide your face from me? From my youth I have been afflicted and close to death; I have suffered your terrors and am in despair. Your wrath has swept over me; your terrors have destroyed me. All day long they surround me like a flood; they have completely engulfed me. You have taken my companions and loved ones from me; the darkness is my closest friend" (Psalms 88)

The dark was comforting and the empty street was too. Susan never remembered getting up and walking back to bed, but the next morning found her in it.

"Because they love me," says the Lord, "I will rescue them; I will protect them, for they acknowledge my name. They will call on me, and I will answer them. I will be with them in trouble. I will deliver them and honor them. With long life I will satisfy them and show them my salvation.

Psalms 91:14-16 New International Version (Paraphrased)

Rescued

"I can't stay in there," Glenn said loudly, complaining about the Rescue Mission program. The sweat was beading up all over his neck and forehead. It seemed a sharp contrast to the coolness of the foggy early morning. His shirt appeared damp halfway down his chest and also on his back when he turned around. His face was pinched and he wore an unnatural expression as he spoke.

Susan thought to herself when does this go away? She wondered if he sweat all night long or was it just when he was awake? She also wondered would he ever get his voice back? Glenn's sudden appearance had surprised his wife. She had just returned to the parking lot after taking the kids to Storyteller. The bus had not moved far these last few days. She had only gone back and forth the short distance from the night spot, but it had been enough to give her some confidence. Right turns were all that were needed in order to negotiate getting into the lot from the railroad tracks, and Jason's services were not yet required. Sitting alone on the steps with the bus door open, she had been trying to decide who could be called to fix the bus. Something had to be done soon. As the designated driver, the task now fell to her of keeping the unmanageable beast running. With Glenn back on the scene, there were now two difficult situations to contend with.

"Why can't you?" she asked, looking at him and trying to readjust her mind to seeing the strange looking man inhabiting the body of her best friend and husband.

"I can't get any sleep in there, Suzi." He paused. "And I got into an argument about a Bible teaching. I couldn't agree with this preacher they brought in there," he said, referring to some part of the mission rehabilitation program. He threw up his hands in exasperation, "You wouldn't believe the nonsense they're teaching people." Glenn laughed as he began to describe in detail the theological discussion that had upset him. He paced back and forth in front of her, agitated and obviously uncomfortable.

As she listened, she prayed to be able to communicate clearly. She was feeling uneasy in his presence, and the way he was acting scared her. The blessed numbness from the shock had not worn off, so the feelings of her wounded heart were protected from responding to any of his pleas.

"Please, honey, let me come home. I need you...I need you all," he begged. "I'm really sorry. I'm sorry for everything."

Susan shook her head. "That's not going to happen, Glenn." She looked around at the empty lot wishing somebody were around. "I told you when we got married I would never tolerate drugs. That would especially include cocaine addiction, don't you think?" She searched his face for a reaction.

"You know I've always said that. This isn't something new," she said firmly hugging her sides with crossed arms for support. "Maybe the Lord wants you to go back to the program and finish it." Resting her head on her knees, she wrapped her arms tightly around tucked-in legs.

Glenn was stunned. This was not the honey he knew, and it definitely was not what he was expecting to hear.

"Maybe He wants to teach you how to put up with things you may not agree with or people you don't like," she continued. "Maybe it would be better than being on the streets trying to figure out how to kick that stuff on your own." Susan stared at the ground and hugged herself even tighter.

"Honey." He stared at her looking bewildered. "You've got to let me come home. I can't make it without you. That's what's wrong with being in the program," he cried, opening his arms and reaching out for his wife. "I said I'd go in a program to get you back, and I did. I'm gonna be all right now. You'll see," he promised.

She leaned away from his embrace. "No!" She ducked from under his arms and leaned forward, stepping outside onto the sidewalk. She stood back from him a few paces, folding her arms across her chest and announced loudly, "For your sake, I wanted you to go through a program. For the sake of your children, I wanted you to go through one. She paused and stared at him for a moment. "Quitting after a few days is nothing."

Glenn slumped down and looked away. "I can't go back," he said hanging his head forlornly. "They said if I walked out that door I couldn't come back. I have nowhere to go. Nowhere! I don't even have a sleeping bag."

She looked at him squarely and said, "I'll give you one."

Glenn's mouth dropped open and he stared at her like she had hit him. Did she remember that was how they first got together? Maybe not. Her words cut deep. "How can you do this to me, Suzi? After all the love I've given you...loved your kids, loved our kids, and now you are treating me worse than a dog." Anger replaced the former pleading in his voice. He shouted, "You'd treat any dog better than you are treating me!"

The truth began to work on her, twisting her insides into a knot. Help me, Lord, she silently prayed. He's getting to me.

"You couldn't have chosen better words, Glenn. That's exactly how I feel for what you did to all of us. Even if you were angry with me for some reason, there will never be an excuse for what you did to your own children. They don't deserve this. How will Holly ever recover? I don't even know where to begin with her, but I know it won't happen if she has to live with someone who can only think about his own needs at the expense of everyone else."

Her words hit a nerve. Raw truth for which he had no solution caused him to realize the justice of his predicament, and Glenn exploded into a rage. "Well, you're not kicking me out! I'm not leaving!" he screamed at her, stomping around and throwing his arms wildly. He pushed past where she was standing and stormed inside. Standing in front of the stove, he grabbed the coffee pot, set it on the stove, then reached over and lit the fire. He grabbed his coffee cup hanging from a nearby hook.

"All right," she responded in a calm voice, shaking inside from fear. She waited, watching him pace. Then he moved to the rear of the bus.

"I built this bus!" he yelled loudly. "This is my bus! No, you leave!" he shouted.

Susan didn't look at him. She was starting to feel again. This time it was anger. Sorry didn't last very long. I know how this turns out, she thought, visiting a memory from her ancient past. I become the bad guy, but I didn't do anything. Sorry doesn't fix lots of things, so I'm sorry too. Sorry that it doesn't.

Glenn continued to rant and rave, slamming cups around and searching for the sugar.

"This is my home I made for this family. I built this bus and you are not going to take it away, Suzi!"

Susan nodded okay, turned and stepped away from the bus. "We'll handle this another way," she whispered.

She walked as though in a dream, looking around and noticing the familiar jungle across the street with its overgrowth of palms. What a day, she thought. Beautiful hibiscus flowers were fragrantly in bloom along the walk and swaying palms were everywhere. The fog had cleared and the sun shone brightly as it nearly always did. The fear began to subside as the moments passed. Looking down at the pavement, she noticed the lines and they reminded her of happy times spent watching her kids playing on their bikes with other homeless kids, sharing time with young struggling families.

She thought about her new friend, Tina, who would always put down safety cones for their babies to crawl around in while they both stood guard. She had instantly loved the family. This place had been their favorite choice for the weekends when the beach lot across Cabrillo was crowded. Most of the RV homeless preferred to park here and not draw extra attention from resentful tourists who wanted to park at the beach. Many made an attempt to disappear on the weekends, but it never mattered. Those who chose to be resentful for whatever reason would remain that way, and homeless preferred to limit their involvement with folks who were easily aggravated. The only fear she had felt before in this place came from the threat of police, but now a greater one was coming from the one whom she had trusted to protect her.

No one was in the lot this Thursday morning to see the tears falling silently down her face. "Thanks for that, Lord." She felt protected by a tender father who had arranged the absence of any witnesses who might increase her shame and embarrassment. The sensation of heaven fell over her shoulders, covering like a blanket and bringing raw emotions instantly into subjection. Feelings once more submerged under God's perfect anesthesia. She swiped at her face with her shirt, and the tears were drying even before she reached the phone booth at the corner of the lot.

"Powerful stuff you got there," she said, looking up at the sky. "I don't know how you do it." She shook her head and turned back to the business at hand.

"911. What is the location and nature of your emergency?"

"I am involved in a domestic dispute, and I live in a two-story school bus parked in the corner lot of Santa Barbara and Cabrillo Blvd. I have asked my husband to leave and he won't. My name is Susan Dunn."

"We will send an officer right over. Will you meet him in the parking lot?"

"Yes, I will." As she hung up, the utter insanity of what she was doing overwhelmed her, and her heart broke for what she knew would happen next. Flashbacks of all they had been through together, the many happy years, all of Glenn's love....all of his love...all of his love. No man had ever loved her before, not once in her life, and Glenn had always given his best. He had shown her what the word family meant, and he had taught her things that would never be forgotten. He had been Christ to her. Yes, he really loved her. What had happened? How could this be true? But she knew these things happened. They always had to her, and now the unthinkable had happened to her Glenn. He was lost to her.

The next few minutes, days, weeks could decide if Caleb and Kelly would know in the future who their parents were. My poor Holly, thought Susan. She started to cry again as two patrol cars pulled into the lot.

She walked briskly toward them and the bus, hearing Glenn yell from inside.

"Oh, God! What has she done now? She's gone and called the cops on me. On me! I can't believe this."

Both cops jumped from their cars and approached her, cutting her off. "Wait here, please." They looked toward the bus. Glenn had stuck his head outside holding up his cup of hot coffee.

"Hello, officers!" he shouted cheerfully.

They nodded toward him, then turned and introduced themselves to her.

"I called you. I'm sorry to have to say that my husband confessed he is a cocaine addict. I was unaware, but now that I know I told him this is not something that I can live with, especially since we are already severely disadvantaged," she said motioning toward the parking lot and pointing at the bus.

"We are not fighting. I love him and always will, but I cannot raise children, be homeless, fight the city and live with a drug addict. I will have to learn to drive this, and I will have to think of what to do next. Right now I am so upset I don't actually feel anything at all." Susan giggled. "I might not be thinking real clear either." She giggled again. "I have to make up...she started to cry but caught her breath...I have to tell the boys a new story. They think their daddy is away getting help because he is sick. They don't know about this. See, he went in the Rescue Mission program for a few days, but he left."

Susan took several big breaths, clenched her fists tightly and regained control. She started to speak again, but in a slow, steady monotone. "I don't...know how...I'm going to tell the boys. They idolize their father. I...did too. I also found out...he hurt our daughter. I have to try...to fix that."

Susan felt courage rising. Finally, she looked at the cop. His eyes were kind and he was holding back tears. Maybe the cops will help, she thought. Maybe one last time. She looked away again and started speaking, "I told him to leave...and he wants me to go instead...but we are homeless. This is our homeless home, and it is quite nice compared to none at all." She was staring at the bus now and nodding, not even seeing her husband waving at them from the steps. "We have a boat right out there," she turned and pointed, "but that didn't work out at all. Maybe he could go out in it."

"My partner will talk to your husband. Wait here with me. Are you all right, Mrs. Dunn?"

"Yeah. He didn't hurt me. I can't believe he would ever do that. But I need help. I just found all this stuff out, and I have to figure out something right away. I know the Lord will help me, but right now I don't have a clue. All that matters at this moment is for the kids to be okay. I have to figure out how to help them through this. Know what I mean?" She stared at the young man again.

He nodded. He did, and he didn't try to hide the sadness he felt, but they both knew this happened every day. This happened to good people who loved each other and loved their families. This happened to people who lived in huge expensive houses, and he had been to them. It happened to those who lived in shacks, but there never were any easy answers. Susan saw in his eyes he had too much experience already with this same situation. Today it happened to the bus family. Today it happened to her.

His partner had a short conversation with Glenn. He wasn't contradicting any of the facts.

"So, you aren't having much success at reconciliation and I

understand you're upset about the threat of losing everything," the tall, dark officer in sunglasses said, resting a hand on his hip. He was gentle, but both officers kept their eyes on Glenn. They had crowded in closely next to him, standing between the couple. "Do you have anywhere you can go right now?" he asked Glenn.

"If I have to I can always find a place to go," Glenn replied, his voice rising. "You can always do something when you have to I guess, but I don't have a sleeping bag or anything. I'm out here on the streets with nothing, like I told you. If we had a home to go to we wouldn't be out here on the streets," his arms flailed as he talked. "Can I ask her for a blanket at least?" He begged, barely looking over his shoulder toward his wife.

"I told him I would give him one," Susan interrupted.

The officer looked at her. "Why don't you go inside and get him what you want him to have. And then, Mr. Dunn," he said turning to face Glenn again, "I want you to leave at this time. These are problems the court will have to decide, but I'm not going to send your wife and children out into the bushes so you can remain inside. You wouldn't really want that for them, now would you?" He gave a piercing man-to-man look to Glenn, and Glenn dropped his head. He looked ashamed.

"No, I wouldn't. I'll leave," Glenn said. "I promise I won't bother her."

"That's good to hear. I don't want to have to come here again when she calls because I've ordered you to stay away, and I don't want to have to make any arrests. You have enough to deal with already I'd think." The officer was skillful. His smooth manner had just handled a delicate situation, one for which the rules were slippery. The home

169

was illegal because it was a vehicle and it had no legal place to be, but it was still a home and they treated it as such.

After Glenn left, the cops stayed for awhile. Susan thanked them and said, "I am going to drive this a short distance away as soon as my son gets home from City College." She looked at the other officer. "Thank you both again for your help. I will always be grateful."

"I'm just sorry," the tall one said as they were driving off. "Let us know if we can help in any way."

Susan knew Glenn would not give up and she would have to face him again. She tried to think of somewhere to go for protection, where she could have people around her for support. The idea of going to the Rescue Mission popped into her head. That was one place he would not want to be near, and she knew they kept security walking the perimeter of the property all night long. She waited until much later after gathering the troops and then prepared for the long journey to the mission four blocks away. Rehearsing in her mind, she thought about the route. There was one left turn out of the parking lot, one right turn, and then two more left turns before parking. Yep, I can probably do it, she thought to herself. Just have to remember not to run over the kiosk center divider again.

A short time later when the family was all gathered together they left the lot without incident, and their new driver felt an inner strength rising. At the first left turn, Jason stepped forward and grabbed the steering wheel, pulling it hard hand over hand until the wheels were properly aligned. His mom drove forward, and they both cheered when it ended up perfectly where she wanted. They did it again at the next left turn.

"Staying on the road," she hollered, "even between the

lines!"

"Nice and steady, Mom. You've got this. Straight ahead now. We're almost there."

Susan was visibly shaking for the next turn onto Yanonali Street, directly in front of the Rescue Mission. "Hope I don't hit anybody. I have to park this thing now."

The curbs were fairly clear and she had a wide choice of spots. She pulled over near the end of the street and was just close enough to be legal, which was good because the bus chose that moment to die.

Jason hopped out and looked at the alignment. "The rear end is sticking out a bit, but I don't think anyone is going to complain." He looked at his mom. She was slumped over the steering wheel, pale and shaking.

"I can't get up. I feel all weak inside."

"You don't have to, Mom. Maybe not for a day or two. You made it."

She smiled weakly. "Lesson completed."

In a few minutes she got up and asked, "Watch these guys for a few minutes, Jason? I've got to talk to someone."

She walked inside to talk about the situation with Matt, the director. She asked him if he would mind her parking nearby on the street and remaining until the bus was fixed. It wasn't safe to drive and even though the old hunk of metal might not seem like much to anyone else it was keeping a leaky roof over their heads and holding all that was precious in their world.

"I don't have any say about the streets," Matt replied. "Most of the time the cops seem to leave people alone who are parked. We can let you use the bathroom and get water, and other than that we can call the police if you have any trouble with Glenn."

"Thanks, Matt," the grateful lady replied. "I didn't know what to do, but I knew the Lord would tell me soon enough. I'm glad to at least have a starting plan. I don't think I'll feel so helpless if I can just learn how to drive the thing. You'll see me practicing at the end of this street, but don't worry. No one is going to get run over down there."

She chuckled to herself and turned to walk out the door, hollering back over her shoulder on the way out, "I didn't even shake that bad when I parked this time, and this is only after my first few tries. I'm just so glad it stopped." Susan thought Matt gave her a funny look as she was leaving but couldn't figure out what it meant.

The following afternoon Glenn paid a visit. Apparently, he had realized the bus wasn't moving from the spot directly in front of the walkway to the mission entrance. Susan had been dreading the next time she would have to talk to him but went outside dutifully when she heard him call to her. She stepped into an ambush of accusations and vicious insults. He exploded with the strength of a firestorm.

"Suzi, this all happened because of you!" Glenn screamed. His voice was coming back. The anger inside had been escalating as his power to control the situation diminished. The things she heard him call her now seemed to be coming out of the mouth of a madman, one Susan had never met. The cloud of sorrow raining down increased exponentially. Grief changed from one of a severe loss to a different type which was more like an inner death. She refused to accept this yelling, screaming person as the one who had been her best friend for so many years.

Obscenities kept pouring from him, one after another, listing the many violations she had committed against their love and against him. Her rejection was now responsible for everything that had ever happened, or so it seemed.

Appearing much like a snarling dog, Glenn had degenerated into a cursing and threatening monster. She stared curiously at him, still trying to figure what alien life form had him.

Susan looked around to see if anyone was aware of what was going on. "I can tell you are very angry with me, but you never called me names before," she said quietly while staring steadily into his face.

"I never thought you would do anything like this to me."

Susan took a step backward toward the open glass doors at the steps. She was afraid because she had no idea what he might do. Several guys had come rushing from around the back of the mission and they were moving toward Glenn, alert and determined. From the corner of her eye she saw a mutual friend of theirs coming from another direction and in the next moment they all converged.

It sounded like they were extending an invitation for him to leave before they called the police. At the first opportunity she jumped out of sight, slamming the doors shut, not wanting to be a part of any more of this disastrous scene. Self-preservation had taken over, shoving years of loyalty from this woman's heart. The slim hope for a future reconciliation was being smashed to powder and thrown to the winds by the demons who were dancing with the crushing of a great love.

Susan knew she was experiencing deep and increasing grief, but all of her feelings were held captive in a state of paralysis. She couldn't cry....she couldn't eat...she couldn't feel. It was the strangest sensation to be walking around in numb-land, but she knew she hadn't swallowed a thing. Medication would not be needed. The Holy Spirit was on the job with some kind of inner protection never felt before, letting the sadness of her wounded soul sink somewhere deep inside. It could all be dealt with later. In the midst of a mighty war, the battles continued to rage. This former Sunday school teacher was now only a foot soldier in the trenches where many had fallen, but the Lord was preparing a path through rocky and dangerous territory ahead.

Several weeks before, Susan had been asked to sing during the evening Rescue Mission service. She had carefully chosen from her many original songs what she would do and had been looking forward to this time when she would finally get to minister to the mission. It had been put on the schedule in the calendar, and it was to be this night. The family was well known by the staff, but Glenn had never been separated from them. It was especially cruel that on this night it would be the first time her mate would not be by her side supporting her. Particularly horrifying was the fact that every man there would be well aware of her crisis, and now she must hold her head high, praise the Lord, and give God the glory.

The buzz permeating her body was a warm blanket of insulation, the God she had always trusted was holding her by his hand, and words of praise easily filled her mouth as she held the microphone up to it. Words of love for her husband, love and gratitude for the mission, but most of all love for the power of God to be with the child he loves in every situation poured from her mouth. Her song was easy and a beautiful testimony preceded it. She did not make light of the tragedy, and she did not accuse or blame anything except the enemy of their souls. When Susan sat down afterward, she was not alone. Grace and mercy walked alongside, shame and guilt had been silenced, and the night spent alone underneath the glaring streetlight was blessed with peace.

Do not fear, for you will not be put to shame, and do not feel

humiliated or ashamed, for you will not be disgraced. For you will

forget the shame of your youth, and you will no longer remember

the disgrace of your widowhood. "For your husband is your

Maker, the Lord of hosts is His name; and your Redeemer is the

Holy One of Israel, Who is called the God of the whole earth. "For

the Lord has called you, like a wife who has been abandoned,

grieved in spirit, and like a wife married in her youth when she is

later rejected and scorned," says your God. "For a brief moment I

abandoned you, but with great compassion and mercy I will gather

you to Myself again."

Isaiah 54:4-8 Amplified Bible

If You See My Kids Will You Tell Them Where The Bus Is?

When the family first moved onto the boat, it was at a time when they had recently changed the church of their attendance, mainly because they felt completely alienated. They had attended this particular church for a couple of years before making the difficult decision to leave, but the girls had begged to be allowed to remain with "their" Sunday school group. Susan remembered how she and Glenn had been torn about what to do, concerned with the effect their decision could have on the girls' tentative developing faith. They finally agreed there wouldn't be a problem with letting them continue. For several weeks the girls had done just that.

Then one day the pastor paid a visit to Glenn's place of work, demanding he not allow their teenagers to take themselves unaccompanied to his church any longer. It wasn't because they behaved badly. He just didn't want the responsibility of minors in attendance without parents. Both parents reacted in shock and rage. Already, they had faced a hard decision and never imagined such a thing could happen in a church. They decided to ignore the pastor's visit after telling him it would hurt their girls too much. They never told the girls. But after he paid a second visit, they realized the girls would do better hearing it from them as opposed to being barred at the door.

They broke it as best they could, but the rejection broke their hearts. It was felt to the core of their being. The looks on their faces had been brutal; no other response could have been expected. Glenn and Susan had hoped they would get over it and try another church. Weeks passed, and they refused to go to any church except for Jennifer and Adolph's youth outreach. It would be the last organized church one of the girls ever went to.

Not realizing the full extent of their trauma, the family attempted to recover and struggled to fit into another church. Although they'd picked a large one, they were never able to connect. They continued to go simply for the fact that Christians go to church. It's what they do. When Susan found herself living alone, she reconsidered.

She thought back to a time when they had first met a street preacher, Dave Hupp, at the Hank and Dave show. This was how the homeless referred to the weekly Sunday service held across the street from the harbor. Brother Hank and Dave faithfully volunteered their time and money for many years. Hundreds would fill the park for breakfast, fellowship, worship, preaching, prayer, lunch, and sometimes clean socks. Dave had introduced himself by handing them a plate of bacon and eggs and inquiring about their needs. He would soon become a close friend, but at the time he had made the suggestion they visit Goleta Vineyard Church. In their precarious position the thought was abhorrent. They were below the first rung of the social ladder in the church world and were too insecure to consider initiating any new relationships. In hindsight, Susan realized staying with a sinking ship hadn't helped anyone. She made the decision to give Dave's recommendation a try.

Goleta Vineyard met at the Hope School every Sunday morning. On her first visit, she came early before service and observed many parishioners working like a team setting up chairs and duct taping heavy cords to the floor. Rolls of tape were consumed weekly to prevent people tripping on the wires coming from the sound boards and other electronics. After service, the same teams worked efficiently to transform the place back into a school. This was a church without a real building, but it didn't stop them in any way from beautiful worship, joyous fellowship, and sound preaching.

Soon after visiting that first Sunday, Susan met and briefly explained her plight to the pastors, hoping for advice and prayer. The pastor prayed, but then he handed her a phone number and asked her to call in a couple of days. He wanted to ask the board what they might be able to do. He wasn't promising anything, but he would let her know.

"Hi, this is the lady who lives in the school bus, Susan Dunn. You said to call?" She felt nervous but didn't know why. She had no expectations and still didn't know what he might have asked the board. After losing her husband, she had left her job and was now receiving welfare, but she had told him that. She also told him the Lord had directed her to start eating lunch at the mission, so they always had plenty to eat. She let him know their basic needs were met and she was capable of managing her affairs, but had no abilities to fix the only thing they had to live in.

"Oh yes, Pastor Dan here. Well, I talked to the board and the church is prepared to offer you some mechanical work on your engine and your brakes. It just so happens we have a mechanic who attends our church, and if I give you his number would you want to call him to see what can be done?"

"Are you kidding? You would do that for me? I mean I could borrow the money, and I would be happy to pay it back a little at a time. That would be wonderful."

"No, you don't have to pay it back. We would like to see what we can do to help," said the kind voice on the other end.

"Praise the Lord!" Susan shouted. "I can't believe it, that you would actually help me like this! Praise the Lord!" She was dazed and unbelieving but quickly wrote down with a shaking hand the name and number which he gave her. "Thank you so much. I have a chance now. Please thank your board for me."

After meeting with the mechanic, the arrangements were made and she went to stay at a young friend's house for a short time. A phone call let her know the bus had two blown head gaskets along with an ailing master cylinder and vacuum booster.

A few days later, Susan sat in the shop of her new friend, listening to all of the good news he had to report. The engine started right up and now performed perfectly. The brakes worked and should give her no more trouble. She was amazed to hear he had even put some 12-volt lights on the bus, a truly precious gift. She giggled with joy at the thought of having light.

"Is there anything else you might need?" he asked.

"Uh...No thank you, but uh..." she looked back at the ancient 1968 relic and quipped, "could you make it last until the boys grow up?"

Then they both laughed and laughed, she believing it could happen through miracles and he shaking his head probably thinking it couldn't.

"There is no way I can tell you how much this means to us. I will remember this forever," she said. "The Lord is using you to save us. Did you know I'm just a new member at Goleta Vineyard? They don't even know me."

"God does," he answered simply.

And so with a heart overfilling with gratitude, driving lessons continued onto new streets. Susan was getting strong enough to make occasional stationary left turns. Sometimes little Kelly would try to help his mom turn the wheel. She mapped out the one-way streets and found times and roads where there was less traffic. Unfortunately, parking was still a problem. The rear corner windows suffered as did a few parking signs. It seemed one had to allow for the overhang turning in three feet when one was exiting. She couldn't quite get the hang of it for well...several signs. Susan hammered boards up in the window to replace the broken Plexiglas.

"I'll just park in the parking lots. I can do those," she said after one oopsie.

"Awe, Mom, you almost cleared it. So close," remarked Kelly.

The townspeople had become extremely friendly to the bus and the people in it. Susan, still terrified of driving, focused intently while behind the wheel and often didn't respond to the constant waves and friendly greetings. She kept Kelly and Caleb near the front as official greeters, and they would wave and cue her in time to give some quick smile or acknowledgment. Folks would later tell her she always looked extremely intense.

"Okay, it's turning yellow. I need to start slowing down." Susan found herself talking through whatever was up ahead. "That car that just jumped in front of me doesn't realize he shouldn't do that in front of big things. Yikes! Praise God for brakes that work. Bless that man, Lord, with wisdom. He's needy. Oh, I feel so bad. I didn't wave at those people back there. They'll think I'm rude, but I have to pay attention or I could crash into something. Oh...they're all so nice and we need all the friends we can get."

"Just drive, Mom," answered Kelly. "We can do this."

Susan smiled fondly at her son. "Kelly, you're so grown up for such a little guy. I'm sorry, honey. You have to do too much. I'm proud of you both, you know that?"

"Pwoud of me," said Caleb.

"Yes, proud of you. You are a good waver."

Another thing had been brought into their lives a few weeks earlier when a big, fluffy dog from the humane shelter had been given as a present to Holly. Susan had hoped it would cheer her up. Holly named him Shadow and seemed quite fond of him at first, trying to train him and spend time with him, but then Susan ended up with...well...a dog.

He rapidly grew bigger and became rather incorrigible. Nobody in the family was much of a dog trainer, which suited Shadow quite well. He established his territory and was more than a handful. He decided his one job in life was to protect the boys (and Susan if she held the leash). This permanently ended any idea of welcoming strangers into the bus, but it made leaving the boys totally safe if she stepped away for a moment. It wouldn't have been any more effective if she had hired a full military guard. Shadow would attack the glass door if anyone made the slightest move toward it, and the boys inside were unable to control or pull him back. This was obvious to anyone considering the risk. Susan came to regard Shadow as backup and referred to him as her angel sent from heaven.

From the time of the traumatic breakup Glenn would show up randomly to visit, always on foot and always chemically altered, yet he seemed much calmer. Usually, he would find his family at the beach lot.

"Came to see my baby boys," he would begin. Then he would try and fail to get his wife to make him a cup of coffee before giving up and going outside to the beach with Caleb and Kelly. "Nobody loves me!" he would say loudly. "Only my baby boys love me."

If someone walked by on the boardwalk, he would often yell, "I made that bus! Yep, that's my bus. That's my family inside. I built it myself." His visits were usually short and Kelly soon refused to go with his dad, but Caleb never.

Susan longed for Glenn to be okay and to be the one he had always been. It was especially cruel that he retained the appearance of the one she loved. "Oh Lord," she prayed. "Isn't there something you can do to give him back to us? Can't you heal him? We need him so much. I need him back."

She begged the Lord constantly, but Glenn wasn't Glenn anymore. Appearances were not deceiving. She knew who her husband was and that man was gone. She owed him everything, but the only thing she could give him now was brief visits with his family.

Life was changing rapidly and she struggled to change with it. Driving lessons were progressing well; other things were not. Both girls had learned their mother stuck to a routine which they could depend on her following. They used her like the city bus and would hop on and off at different points in town. Although it was a small town, this drove Susan nuts. She was already losing her girls, and this was just another way that left her feeling out of control. She had put both of them in Santa Barbara schools while Jason was going to City College. Caleb had special needs and she had put him in Head Start. Kelly was the only one who remained in home school. Their home was once more a school bus even if for a brief period of time, and a lot of driving was required to keep up with all the daily pickups and drop offs.

"Hey!" a stranger popped up to the driver's window at a red light. "Jackie said if I saw the bus I should tell you she will meet you at the wharf in an hour."

"Uh, what? Uh, thanks. Thanks a lot," a bewildered mother stared at the stranger.

Another time, turning down Victoria Street both girls came running from the curb. Their mom slowed to nearly a stop and opened the door while they jumped on. "We were on our way home, but you beat us there." They both got the giggles over the clever play on words.

"Be more careful or I will run over your toes next time."

"Mom, go down State Street, please?" the girls begged.

It was a terrifying thought, but Susan was so happy to have her girls home and safe that she decided to do it.

"Once I get on I have to stay all the way to the beach, you know?"

State Street was the cruising street anytime day or night and it was always packed. The fact that driving would be at a crawl was comforting so Susan put it in low gear and moved like a float in a parade. They were exactly that. The sidewalks were lined with crowds, fingers pointed, and everybody was waving and talking about the bus. Movie stars walked with tourists on the sidewalks, and cars only the very rich could own were in the parade with her. Some had names she couldn't even pronounce. She wondered if her insurance was enough to cover a fender bender for some of the vehicles surrounding her.

"Okay, just stay calm," Susan spoke quietly. "I can do this,

Lord. I can do this. Drive and smile at the same time, yep. Oh my, we are actually taking this monstrosity on State Street. Okay, guys, I'm ready for new things. Beverly Hillbillies just arrived, peoples, and I have on my floppy hat to prove it. Oh yeah...okay, gotta stay calm."

"Oh, Mom! You are talking to yourself. You're so silly," said Jackie. "Hey, we are on State Street. We really are."

It was exhilarating to finally make it to the beach and escape the limelight, but it was even more wonderful to experience the feeling of belonging somewhere, a relatively new thing in this woman's life.

There were many times when she would pull up at a red light and friendly people, some she knew and some she didn't, would tell her where the girls were and when they would be at the wharf. Some would tell her they needed to be picked up at a certain location. Others just let her know what the girls were doing and that they were fine. On occasion the schedule would have to be changed. It didn't happen often but when it did it was terrifying.

"Hey, Jeff. If you see the girls, will you tell them I am going to be late getting back?"

On another corner, "Hey, Amy, if you see the girls, will you tell them I won't be on time? Just tell them to wait for me a little bit, okay?"

"Mom, someone needs to invent a phone like on Star-Trek. Then we wouldn't have these problems," piped up Kelly one day. "When I grow up I'm going to invent a laser phone."

"Good idea, but I'm afraid it isn't going to happen in our lifetime, at least not while we need it."

"Well, when I grow up you will have it," he assured her.

One dark and cold night the kids all arrived late and hungry at Stearns Wharf parking lot and almost at the same time. Jason had just come from his job and realized dinner could take a long time, so he offered to buy everyone a huge pizza.

"That's nice, Jason, but how far is a pizza place from here? I never went to one yet so I don't know about parking, but I guess I could circle the block while you get it."

"No, Mom. I'm going to go across the street to the phone booth and order one delivered." He looked quite happy with the idea.

"No, way! You think they would even consider coming out to a dark, empty parking lot in the cold with take-out?"

"I'm sure I could talk them into it," he answered. "They should have no trouble finding us. We are one of a kind, you know?"

"I never heard of such a thing." His mom was not nearly as confident as he.

"Do it, Jason!" a chorus of voices erupted as he marched briskly across the street, pulling his jacket up close around his neck in the biting wind. A few moments later he returned.

"Well, it was rather entertaining there for a moment, but we should have a pizza in about fifteen or twenty minutes."

Cheers went up in eager anticipation.

"They said they had never delivered to a bus in a parking lot before. I described our bus, and I told him nothing else comes close to looking like us. I have the money and lots of hungry brothers and sisters. He seemed a little bit afraid of getting in trouble, but I am pretty sure I talked him into it." Jason's whole face glowed with satisfaction. "Also, I have a nice tip for when he comes."

Jackie reached over and gave him a spontaneous hug. "Thanks. We never get pizza."

The kids followed their big brother outside hoping to catch a glimpse of the pizza man, but the cold sent most of them quickly running back. Anticipation was high, there were lots of giggles, and a party was in the air, but Susan worried what she would do if he didn't come. It was unreasonable to expect such a thing from a business. She was beginning to think she should drive them somewhere when the glare of headlights spun around in her face through the bus window. She watched Jason reach down and complete the transaction through the car window so the fellow didn't even have to get out in the cold. His eyes were open wide as he stuck his head outside and craned his neck, taking in the entirety of the huge, wooden vehicle in the pitch black of night. She saw handshakes and big smiles before the white Pinto spun off as quickly as it arrived.

Jason burst through the door with a celebratory swoosh and bow. "Dinner has arrived. Dig in, guys."

Shouts of praise erupted then ceased almost as quickly as the pizza began to disappear with the speed of vultures attacking carrion.

"He really liked the bus," Jason said in between mouthfuls, "and he said he was sure glad it wasn't a prank. He would have gotten in a lot of trouble. We can do this again. Oh, by the way, Mom. I have been meaning to ask you. Would you care if I rented a limousine and took the girls one night to cruise the Hollywood Strip? Some guy has a limo business and he owes me for some work I did for him, so I thought I would take a trade. I will keep 'em in the car and nothing will happen to them. I promise. I think it would be fun to get picked up in this parking lot in a big, black, stretch limo, go up and down State Street, and drive around all night. Don't you?"

Jason stopped long enough to look up at his mother, who

was staring back at him speechless, her hand froze mid-air with a partial slice of pizza, her mouth open in disbelief. "Wha...You want to do what with the girls?"

Speak up for those who cannot speak for themselves; ensure justice for those being crushed. Yes, speak up for the poor and helpless, and see that they get justice.

Proverbs 31:8-9 New Living Translation

Birth of an Activist

911. It is a number even small children know how to call. Anyone who might ever need to dial it would expect an immediate response to their cry for help. Susan was convinced that 911 would never refuse to respond to anyone. A strange set a circumstances enlightened her.

Undoubtedly tapes are kept of such things, but this would be one incident that would invite itself to be erased. Police also keep detailed notes of their activities, but not necessarily the scraps of paper they are written on. Somewhere under God's heaven there is a record attesting to the veracity of the events as they unfolded, but where it would be now is unknown. What is known is that during this particular moment in time a group of public servants worked together to deal with an unusual situation. What they chose to do produced another public servant who would become dedicated to speaking for all the ones who had no voice. She would have voted herself as most unlikely to consider such a challenge, but the passion ignited lit an unquenchable fire. It would burn hot, refusing to dissipate and only grow in intensity as the days continued.

It had been a celebratory time. The Goleta Vineyard church had invited everyone to a Good Friday service to be held at the Santa Barbara High School auditorium. This, the highlight of the Christian year, had everyone excited, and many other churches had been included in the invitation. Susan inquired about access to the parking lot and had been assured she could easily get the bus in. The girls had gone with their youth group to a weekend retreat, and Glenn was a few towns away at his sister's house. There should be no problems.

"Celebrate, Jesus, celebrate," Susan sang to herself, glancing at the clock. Still morning, she thought. She wished she could feel more inspired over teaching times-tables and English literature.

"Write it one more time. You are doing well." She stole another glance at the clock. "Now for reading," she announced. Just stay focused, she encouraged herself. Two more hours and we'll all be free.

The bus would be traveling a different route to get to the high school, but it wasn't far. Mentally, Susan rehearsed the road. Every new place she considered driving was stressful to contemplate. She hummed another song while she warmed up some spaghetti, then threw together a snack meal of peanut butter crackers, grapes, and avocados to be eaten later, bagged it and stuffed it on top of the counter. Planning ahead was a sure way to be free for the rest of the afternoon and evening.

The basic necessities in the bus were wearing thin on this day, and their facilities were in dire need of servicing. Saturday morning was her designated day for getting water, dumping the porta-potty, buying groceries, ice, and doing laundry. Her day of chores had been chosen to coincide with the one day when she could take advantage of the boys' desire to watch cartoons. She was stretching it this week, though and she knew it. Laundry cascaded unconstrained over the box and onto the floor, the potty was almost maxed out, and most of the food was gone. Glaring at the two nearly empty Sparklett's bottles, she realized they were at critical mass, but the present excitement overrode any concerns for survival needs. We'll make it, Lord, she thought. Praising the Lord with all of your heart—a real celebration is what the pastor had said, and she was ready to party! Her thoughts were interrupted by a small voice.

"School's over, Mom. I'm done," Kelly announced joyfully. He slammed his math book shut and looked at her from his lofty perch over the driver's seat. Grabbing the door frame with one arm, he swung his legs out through the two-square-foot opening, twisted his body 180 degrees around and artfully caught his foot on the pivot handle attached to the glass doors. This well-rehearsed movement appeared to be beautifully choreographed. It was more impressive that Kelly never missed. His other foot slid quickly along the three-foot metal arm attached to the door, guiding him for a moment before he gently glided onto the floor. His arms went up as though he had just made a basket on the court, then he leaned back and reached over to grab an apple on the counter. Susan never looked up but heard the crunch of the apple, its fragrance quickly filling the air.

"Get things ready to go, boys," she announced joyfully. "Get the dog in and the buckets. We're out-a-here!"

They were early. They had to be. It was critical to getting a place to park. Parking, however, proved to be as easy as had been reported. Kelly gave the bus door the typical slam to lock it, and they all stepped out into a golden tapestry of warmth from the sunbeams, blue sky, and gorgeous spring blooms dotting the campus. Susan felt chilled and began to feel unusually tired as they walked toward the building. Walking across the immaculate campus with the beautiful rose garden in the quad, a pressure was building inside her head and a sensation of weakness. Her jacket was not helping with the chills.

"It's time to start praising the Lord!" Mumbling much quieter, she added, "That's my prescription anyway to snap out of this."

Susan stumbled as she struggled to make her way up the stairs into the building. Unaware of the degree that her coordination was rapidly deteriorating, she staggered like a drunk. She tried to shake it off, to push through it with the excitement for the evening and override any normal reactions to symptoms now mounting a full assault. Ugly sensations that Susan was unwilling to acknowledge were invading.

"Hold my...hand...Caleb." Her voice was slurred and thick. Concentrating on the words, her mouth wouldn't form the sounds properly. "I don't want...to have...to chase around...to...find you."

But Caleb had been holding onto his mom. He was rarely seen in public not attached to her in some way. Constantly worrying about what might happen next, she was a mother who nagged her boys about every possible thing that could befall them. Like a frightened bird, this mother hen kept trying to account for her straying chicks and at the present time she was down to two.

"I'm feeling funny. I want you both to stay right next to me, okay?"

Both boys nodded and moved closer to her, wanting to help in some way. Once inside the huge, crowded and darkened amphitheater, they walked into a wall of sounds filling every particle of space as a sea of uplifted hands and voices joined the rock band in a roaring crescendo. They made their way to three seats in the middle section. Space and time stopped for her as Susan longed to jump in and melt into it, but the weakness was not going away as she had hoped. Instead, it was growing to the point where sitting was her only option. They sat quietly for a few songs, swallowed by the standing crowd while she felt the loud music reverberating through her head. The pressure increased with each beat.

Susan leaned over and shouted into Kelly's ear. "I've got to get out of here. I've got to lie down." She grabbed Caleb's hand and stood. "Come on, Cabe. We have to go now."

"Too soon, Mommy," he whined.

"Something's...wrong...with my...head, honey." She struggled to speak clearly. "Come on!" She tugged on his hand and led him through the crowd. There was a rushing need to escape, an overwhelming feeling of wanting to hide in the way of a wounded animal. As they made their way to the bus, she found herself swaying and stumbling across the lot.

"Oh, it's so far away. Guys, if I can just lie down for a little while I think everything will be okay," Susan tried to reassure. "We'll leave to go back to Mark's yard in an hour or so as soon as I can drive."

Her legs began to buckle and the bus was still too far away. Kelly tried to hold onto his mother and help her. Both boys were worried. Shadow watched them approach, jumping against the glass door of the bus and wagging his whole body. He was always overjoyed to see his pack return.

"There is enough juice in the battery for awhile," Susan said as she climbed into the darkened interior. "Why don't...you guys...watch TV?" she stammered and bumped into the cabinet. Hearing a muffled reply, she turned.

"What?" It was the last thing spoken before collapsing onto the floor cushions in the rear of the bus. She laid there listening to a loud roaring sound in her head, the pressure building inside and quickly throwing her down, deep into unconsciousness. Susan whispered, "Lord, maybe I should get help."

"Hey! Anybody in there? I'm locking up!" a man's loud voice startled Susan out of the deep stupor.

"Wait!" She hollered in a voice intended to be a shout but hadn't managed to squeak any louder than a whisper. How had everything gotten so black, and where was she anyway?

"Wait!" she tried again. This time, it was a bit louder, almost a squawk. Crawling on her hands and knees, she aimed where the door should have been. The dog was barking furiously through the glass at the man.

"You people staying all night?" the voice shouted again. The sound was coming from within an idling vehicle right outside the bus.

"No!" she shouted. "Wait!" The pressure inside her head had complete control of her senses.

She continued to crawl to the sound of the engine outside and then managed to stand by holding onto the sink. She hit the glass with her fist in the direction of the blinding headlights, and it bounced off barely as a tap. A man had his head sticking out of a rolled-down car window. Blackness was all around, so black that even the color of his car wasn't something she could recognize. She wasn't sure she could see him either, but she could hear him. Shaking on wobbly legs that were refusing to hold her steady, she leaned over the counter to keep from falling.

"Last call if anyone is in there. I've got to go," he yelled as he started to drive off.

"Wait, please. We're leaving." Susan cried in a tiny, weak voice, as she stumbled to the front, frantically searching for keys. "What is wrong with me?" she said out loud to a silent bus. "I'm acting worse than a drunk."

Everything moved in slow motion, and Susan wondered how she would be able to drive when she couldn't even walk. Her arms felt like heavy wooden clubs, and her fingers were deadened and unresponsive as she dug into the jacket hanging on the driver's seat. The keys were in there, but then she couldn't get them into the keyhole. It had to be the right key, or was it? She looked hard at the set of keys in her hand. Reaching over and pulling on the headlights gave a dim light. The interior, green panel lights cast an eerie pale glow, but the light wasn't helping much. She felt suddenly stupid. None of the keys she was staring at would tell her which one went to the ignition. This had never before been a problem.

"Please, Lord, help me get this thing started. Keep that man waiting for me, please. Surely he can see I'm trying to get out of here. God, please help!" she prayed.

It felt like a dream of running underwater and getting nowhere, or was it a dream? One key seemed more familiar, and she fumbled trying to point it in the right direction. Using shaking hands to guide the key, the bus slowly roared to life. The old metal and wooden turtle crawled out of its space, lumbering the short distance around the circle lot to the entrance.

"Oh, no!" Two closed, black, wrought-iron gates stood in front of her as sentries with arms locked together. Shivering violently now and feeling very weak, she was grateful the boys had put themselves to bed long ago. They were mercifully unaware of their predicament. "Where did the man go?" She stared at the gates for a long while, waiting for him to reappear.

"It must be you, Lord. The way I feel I shouldn't be driving anything right now. What is wrong with me anyway?" she muttered shaking her head, trying to push the panic away. "I'll call someone in the morning for help. No

197

use trying to get someone out of bed tonight." It was late enough that no cars were on the road, but the wall clock was hidden in the deep shadows and unreadable at the moment. She worried if the boys were okay about having to put themselves to bed but worried more about how long before this feeling would go away. Everything needed to be all right again. As she began to make her way, she tripped halfway back to the cushions and the darkness wrapped its arms around all of the confusion, shutting everything out and surrounding her senses once again with numbing blackness.

The brightness of the rising sun woke the kids, and they scurried to the morning appointment with Saturday cartoons. "Mom, start the bus," they begged, tugging on her shirt. If they thought anything was unusual about their mother lying on the floor, they gave no evidence.

"Caywub needs mo battewy. Pwease wake up and stawt da bus, okay?" Caleb begged again.

"Huh? What's going on?" their surprised mother mumbled as she struggled to sit up. Whoa...here we go again, she thought as the walls spun around her. "Yeah, okay guys. Just a minute." She stumbled to the driver's seat in an effort to start the bus.

"Boy, do I need coffee or something." Susan listened to the purr of the engine for a few moments, then stood and made her way to the counter. While standing at the stove making coffee, she thought over what had happened the night before. Glancing down, she saw that powdered milk had been spilled everywhere on the counter. It was evidence the boys had managed to get their own breakfast. She noted ruefully that it was going to take a lot of scrubbing to get the hardened, sticky stuff off.

"Guys, I'm going to get us out of here. Stay inside!" she ordered as she left the bus and made her way to the pay phone located in front of the school office. Walking through the well-kept rose garden with the fragrance filling the morning air, Susan took a deep breath letting it fill her senses. "Just how does one begin to get oneself out of a situation like this?" she mused. She kept hoping the coffee would do its magic and she could snap back to normal at any moment. The day was brilliant with promise, chores were calling, and she was confident they would be getting out of this confinement quickly. Life had taught her not to expect or demand very much from anyone, so she planned to keep her requests as minimal as possible.

The first call to 911 was presented as a request for advice. "I'm locked inside a schoolyard, and I need to get out. Who should I call?" Susan asked calmly.

The lady on the other end was polite and understanding and immediately gave her a number to the business office.

Plink, plink, went the quarter. "Hello. I'm trapped inside a schoolyard, and I'm trying to figure out how to get out," she repeated, trying to sound as pleasant as possible, but her head once again felt like it was going to explode with pressure.

After listening to the description of how it all happened, a voice on the other end said, "I'm sorry. It's the weekend and it will cost overtime for us to call someone to let you out."

There was a long pause on Susan's end. This did not compute and she stood staring at the phone shaking her head. Then words came. "What do you mean?" Susan cried, her voice rising. "We can't stay in here all weekend. I've got two kids and we need water. We need bathroom facilities and food. I need to get medical attention. Whatever happened to me last night that made me pass out is still happening. I can't believe you are going to leave me here all weekend. I need to see a doctor!" Susan shouted into the receiver.

"I'm sorry," came the reply.

Hanging up in a fury, Susan called a series of numbers and got an equal number of negative answers or just recorded messages. An uncontrolled shaking now accompanied the other symptoms. Her face had drained of all color, and the feeling of helplessness was overpowering. She felt like she was going to faint and lost the ability to control her voice or manifest any volume. A quiet, flat monotone was all that would come out.

"911, emergency," said a pleasant voice again.

"I'm the one who called a few minutes ago, and the police are refusing to help. They won't send an officer to respond for any reason, and I begged them to. Look, I need to get out of here." Woozy, her legs buckled from under her and she slumped silently to the ground. "I don't know what's wrong with me, but I need to get medical attention! We're homeless. We live in a bus and we can't stay here all weekend." She began to ramble, taking quick breaths in between words. "I can't believe...you won't help me. I need...help. I really need help from...somebody."

"I'm very sorry. There's nothing I can do," the voice was apologetic.

Susan detected something else in her voice. She couldn't define it. Was it embarrassment or pity? She wasn't sure exactly.

"You say you live in your R.V. Why don't you go lie down for awhile and see if you feel better?" The dispatcher spoke gently, almost as though she were speaking to a child.

"No!" came the firm retort. "I need to get to a doctor! Something is really wrong! If you'll just let me out, I'll get to my own doctor if I have to. Please!" she begged. "I can't believe I'm calling 911 and no one will come."

Stunned, Susan hung up the receiver not knowing what to do next. She barely made it back to the bus before collapsing on the stairs inside. Sitting there holding her head, she tried to keep the walls from spinning. The tears began to fall and her nose started to drip, but she refused to give in to sobs, taking slow, deep breaths. The boys had never seen their mother cry. The garbage sack odors and the smell of the overfilled porta-potty swirled around her, laughing and taunting in the predicament. Susan sensed Caleb walking her way and reached over and snatched a hanging towel to hide her face.

"When ah dey goin to unwock da gate, Mommy?" he asked quietly.

Her voice was slightly muffled from talking through a towel, and she used few words to explain what was happening. "Nobody will come. They said they can't come for two days." Then she added, "I need a guardian angel to bring me a hacksaw, and I will get that lock off! I will get us out of here. You hear that, Lord?" She shouted up at the ceiling. "If you got any angels to spare I sure could use one right now."

A few minutes passed while she sopped up tears with the dish towel and gulped slow, deep breaths, coping with a sea of rage. Her mind took turns envisioning a couple of scenarios. In one, she saw herself ramming the gate like a crazy woman, and in the other, she saw an angel dressed in street clothes walking up and handing her a hacksaw. Susan became uncomfortable with the crazy woman vision; it was a little too scary.

A knock on the bus startled Susan from her fantasies. "Alan!" she shouted. A chorus of Alans and whoops could be heard from the boys. "How did you ever find us?"

"Well, I remembered you said you were going to be here yesterday, and when you weren't in the yard or any of the usual places I figured I'd come back here to start looking. You know, you are kind of hard to hide." He wore his typical smirk.

"Alan, today you are an angel." she gushed, filled with relief. "Did you know that? I prayed for an angel and look what the Lord sends. I can't believe it. He really does listen to me. So, do you know where we can find a hacksaw?"

"It just so happens I have one in the back of my car," replied Alan. He quickly returned with the necessary implement and in moments the chain hindered them no longer.

Joy over this new turn of events gave her strength to attempt the escape. "Alan, something is really wrong, but if I can just get this back to the yard then I can think about getting to a doctor."

Mark's yard was a place of business across the street from the beach and hidden by "the jungle". Mark was the son of a politician and a landscaper by trade. He sold soil amendments which was basically another word for dirt, many kinds of dirt, and they were all special. He had graciously offered Susan a refuge at night and on weekends inside his barbed-wire fenced enclosure. In return, he wanted night security for his business and that became Shadow's job. Susan had the use of a phone and an office while there, but most important for her it was a safe place to hide. She found herself going there more and more.

"I'll follow right behind," Alan offered.

"That would be a good idea. I'm feeling a little stronger, but things are still not right."

They pulled out of the lot and slowly rounded the Anapamu corner onto Milpas Street. They had only gone a block more when several patrol cars began following. A few blocks later red lights flashed in the bus mirrors, and Susan quickly pulled over on lower Milpas adjacent to the freeway. She jumped off the bus to greet two officers standing right outside. The short one started saying something about he knew what she had done and he didn't blame her for it, but...

"Why didn't you come?" she shouted at him. She was furious when she realized why they had pulled her over. "I needed your help. I was trapped and I called 911. They told me to just go lie down when I said I needed medical help. You wouldn't come. I can't believe nobody would come."

The officer asked for her license and name, scribbling down the information in his little tablet, and then stated the school might want to charge her for another chain.

"I don't think they will press charges," he added.

Susan became incensed as the full impact of his words sunk in. "They said no officers could come out on the call to rescue me, but look how many will come for a broken chain." She waved her hands toward the many squad cars pulled over and now parked behind the bus. "I can't believe you're stopping me for rescuing myself. I bet you guys were listening the whole time when I was calling the police and begging 911 for help, but you wait until I escape to show up?" Her voice had risen in pitch and volume. Furious with rage, she cried, "Why didn't you come when I needed you?"

Susan was so angry she couldn't stop trembling. "Before today, I always believed that when people call the police for help they come, but you didn't. I just don't understand." She fought to control the tears threatening to betray her and put her in a position of weakness.

"So you're willing to accept full responsibility for breaking out and damaging school property?" The officer squirmed in the face of the scathing tirade. He looked to the other officer standing nearby, but his partner offered no help, turning away from his glance.

"Yes, of course. It would be a privilege to buy the school another piece of chain. Where do I sign?" she snapped at him while grabbing his pen and scribbling where he pointed.

Her anger had served one purpose. It gave her another burst of strength to finish driving the next few blocks to the yard. Once back inside Mark's compound, she turned the key off, walked back to the cushions, and remembered turning the boys over to Alan's care just before crashing into another comatose stupor.

I've got to call a doctor, she thought. The last sounds heard were of Alan and the boys wrestling outside with the dog barking. Caleb was laughing, someone else was yelling, then everything went black.

Susan awoke to the late afternoon sun and stumbled around to get up and make her way outside. A note on the door let her know Alan had taken the boys to get something to eat. She needed to use the phone in the office and stumbled out to call the doctor. An answering machine informed her the clinic was closed until Monday.

Confused, her decision-making capabilities were seriously impaired and the 911 incident had been traumatizing. She contemplated calling an ambulance but couldn't face another ordeal of rejection and refusal. Everything inside of her wanted to go to the hospital, but in her stupor she imagined it must be God's will she stay away from doctors. She retreated back to the cushions.

It was most fortunate the symptoms began to subside on their own the following day. The overwhelming feeling of pressure in her head had lessened, and she was able to walk better. On Resurrection Sunday, strength was coming back into her body and things were improving considerably. There were many hours to wait until Monday, and on Monday she wasn't able to be seen until Tuesday. What exactly happened those four days will never be known. Immediate medical attention might not have made any difference, but some kind of cerebral incident occurred, leaving behind lingering and insidious disabilities.

In addition to the circumstances that the family had come to live with, there now would be added an additional complication threatening them much more than the police, the community, or the laws prohibiting their existence. This Easter weekend would begin a frightening, new journey testing Susan to the extreme limit of her ability to endure. There would follow constant trips to the doctor, medical tests, and treatment plans over a period of months and years, all proving futile until eventually a medication would be found allowing her to heal. Long before that day arrived, however, she would need to perfect her techniques in ducking and hiding from a mounting number of adversaries. Most importantly, she would need to succeed in keeping her condition a secret and train the boys to remain inside at all costs whenever the near daily bouts of unconsciousness occurred.

Another change of profound significance also occurred

that weekend. She had always believed if one stayed as invisible as possible on the streets by not causing any problems, then the ruling authorities would grant some grace and leave those individuals alone. The truth was so different from her naive misconceptions. There were no good guys, there were no innocents, and the vulnerable were only easier targets.

Something in the newspaper...she struggled to remember what it was. She had read about some kind of a homeless protest at City Hall and remembered thinking before that the ones who behaved like that were wrong. They were troublemakers, those ones who acted up in public, and if you behaved like that it would only make people dislike you. That's what she had thought. Protesting—wasn't that something radicals and revolutionary-type people did? Sensible, law-abiding citizens should never approve of such counterproductive tactics.

Boy, was I wrong about that, thought Susan. There were good reasons for what they were doing. Never before had it been this clear what the founding fathers were thinking when they gave citizens the Bill of Rights. In high school, she had won the Constitution essay contest two years in a row, but that didn't help her now. She couldn't even remember what most of those rights were. At this moment there was one thing she knew was certain. Some of hers had just been violated.

Frantically, she searched through the growing stack of old newspapers beside the trash. Thinking it was a fairly recent story, she was hopeful it had not yet been tossed. Susan pounced on a picture staring at her. Here it was, the story about the homeless. Yes, she was reading the same words, but now the story read differently. Everything was different now.

This rag-tag, wounded army of disenfranchised citizens were the only ones who had nothing more to lose. Alone and abandoned, these protesters were willing to stand against the terrible, daily injustices and demand their God-given, human rights. The struggle might appear to be their own, but everyone's freedom was at stake. Their humble request was not a demand. They were merely asking for permission to continue to exist.

Susan resolved to go to the City Hall immediately. There was a hunger growing inside of her to know these people. She made a decision to join them.

For we wrestle not against flesh and blood, but against

principalities, against powers, against the rulers of the darkness of

this world, against spiritual wickedness in high places.

Ephesians 6:12 King James Version

Caleb Disappears

One time Caleb vanished into thin air. He wasn't misplaced or left somewhere, but he simply disappeared. He was put to bed one night and in the morning he was gone. It was one of God's miracles he was ever returned.

Since joining the City Hall protests, Susan had met many new friends who came from all walks of life. She met Nancy and Bob, dedicated Santa Barbara activists, Crazy Ed and his dog, Jeff Hess, the lovable schizophrenic cartoonist, Kim and her children, and Will Hastings, a top level attorney who would become her greatest ally. There were so many new people in her life. Homeless advocates poured in from all over the country, adding to the faithful few holding down the "concrete fort" on the steps of the City Hall building. With each day that passed, the protest grew in intensity and it captured the attention of the national news media.

The previous evening had been interesting. Susan liked to park the bus directly in front of the steps each night so the kids would feel she was close to them. When they weren't climbing the big tree in front or balancing on the iron rails at the steps with their new friend, Krystal Freedom, they preferred staying inside watching TV or amusing themselves in some other way while they waited for their mom. On this particular evening, Susan had decided to bring her guitar out on the steps, and there she sang praise and worship at the top of her lungs until after ten o'clock.

Earlier around nine o'clock Kelly had announced, "You guys have fun. I'm going to bed." With that, he marched the few steps over to the bus, hopped up into his cubicle, and tucked himself in for the night. Susan had watched him as he pulled his feet up inside and then slam the little wooden door shut. Caleb followed after his brother and grabbed his blanket and pillow. He returned and plopped down beside his mom. The little guy was like a koala bear on a tree, attaching himself to his mom wherever she went.

"When I can't see you, I know you're there...When I can't feel you, I will not fear...I will trust in you and I will not be afraid," Susan sang out loudly as she did every night, selecting many songs from her overstuffed bag. Most nights she sang from behind a curtain of walls. The cold steel panels kept no secrets as even quiet voices reverberated inside, amplifying their sound.

Susan's stage performer's voice carried freely as she belted out unreservedly "...nothing but the Blood of Jesus," and "...You are my hiding place, you always fill my heart with songs of deliverance, whenever I am afraid, I will trust in you."

But this night had been different. This night the stars could clearly be seen and it was crisp and cool, too beautiful not to be admired. What drew her outside, though, were the faces of the people gathered on the steps. They seemed forlorn and broken. They regarded their government as a benevolent parental unit who should provide a direction for them to walk toward other than simply "get out of town". At the very least, they wanted better advice. Susan saw them clustered together in sad little groups, often hungry and dirty, wearing ragged, inadequate clothing while trying their best not to complain about the discomfort. Humble to the extreme, they appreciated all of the crumbs that fell to them from the Master's table.

"Hey, I don't know what I'm gonna do. They said I can't

go there anymore. They said they don't want me bothering the tourists." The stout, short, red-haired lady with an extreme amount of poorly, applied makeup appeared from out of the shadows. She stood bawling like a five-year-old standing on the sidewalk. "That's not fair! That can't be right, can it?" She screeched in a strange, unnatural voice. Cheeks hung out of the bright, pink short-shorts and beginning to shiver in the skimpy, white, sleeveless shirt, she appeared to be in her thirties or maybe even older. Her arm brushed the matted, curly hair from her face, smudging her makeup horribly into a contorted, clownish appearance. Many of the homeless rolled their eyes or looked away when they noticed her. She was the type who upset even the most tolerant group of people in the world. She was a real case.

Two men surrounded her and began to "take care of it". It was a job that fell to many in the camps, and they were used to handling the worst of the worst.

"Shut her up! Get her out of here!" Two or three angry men bellowed out.

Another man buried in his sleeping bag alongside the sidewalk reared up from a deep sleep. "What's going on? Hey, who's hurt? What the…"

The self-appointed caretakers put their arms around her and walked her away from the main group and over to the grassy area in the park across the street.

"She can't be around here! She'll ruin things for all of us!" a voice continued to yell. "Stacey, stay away from here! I'm telling you that you have to stay away!"

"Hey, I'm just as homeless as you are!" she screamed at the top of her lungs. "You don't own the world!" she retorted emphatically with a few spicy adjectives.

"I got it, man. Don't worry. We can take care of it," came

the reply from one of Stacey's comforters. And they did. One of them walked her off, but many quieter ones remained. These too were taken care of by those who realized their duty to their fellow man, respecting the dignity of anyone's humanity.

One quickly got the impression these were all dependent children who for one reason or another couldn't accept the fact they had been orphaned. Sadly, they did not realize they weren't very good at taking care of themselves. Too ugly and too old to be adopted, they were stubborn in their insistence that someone should care. It was impossible for Susan to perceive them as the threat that others envisioned.

Whenever the night shadows fell, Caleb's usual habit was to grab a sleeping bag and whimper relentlessly for his mother to come inside for the night so he could go to bed. He was very good at getting her to quit whatever she was doing, ending the day for all. This night was different. Maybe it was just too pretty outside or the people too needy, but Susan persisted in sitting down and singing with all her heart as unto the Lord. The presence of the Holy Spirit surrounded everyone, and people began commenting on the strange physical sensations they were experiencing.

"Oh, I just got the chills all over when you sang," Julie ran up to her, the forty-ouncer in her hand nearly drained. "I got the chills right now!" she repeated. The short, friendly lady always wore a black bandanna around her brown, chopped hair and deep sores covered her face. Julie was fighting the demon of AIDS and the fear of its power to take her life. Her husband had recently died of it, and she had a small boy who she would be powerless to protect after she soon would leave the earth. The panic eased with her own brand of self-medication.

"I'm not religious, but I feel like God is so real right now," she held out her arms filled with scabs and sores, looking at them in wonder. "I do. Look at this! Look at these goose bumps! I feel chills all over me." Tears poured down her chubby cheeks as she looked up at Susan, her face glowing.

"That's the Holy Spirit, Julie. God loves us all so much. He wants us to be able to feel him," she whispered quietly.

"Oh, it must be true," Julie continued to cry. "You know I have AIDS. I'm gonna die of AIDS." She was loud, her voice rising with emotion.

"Well, now you know God is not worried a bit about it. He is letting you know you are very special. Julie, he absolutely wants you to know you are loved," Susan said, leaning on her guitar and staring at Julie and the group of friends around her.

"Sing some more, oh sing some more," Julie begged while crying and trying to sing along.

"What can wash away my sin?...Nothing but the Blood of Jesus. What can make me whole again?...Nothing but the Blood of Jesus". As Susan sang, all the people joined in and everyone "got the chills". Everyone except for one little half-sleeping boy lying against his mother's leg.

"Mommy, please come inside. I want to go to bed. Please, Mom," Caleb begged.

"No, I'm not ready yet. Just lay down and go to sleep, honey. You'll be all right. I'll carry you inside so you don't need to worry." She reached down and covered him better, patting his back to reassure him. The singing and praising continued for several minutes longer, then Susan got up and put everything away into the bus. Friendly hands helped her get a drowsy boy in his bed, and she drove off late in the evening to one of their nesting places near the railroad tracks.

She put the locking bar on the handle, checked on the two sleepers behind the little wooden doors, and crawled up into her loft. She must have fallen asleep around eleven, but sometime later Susan was awakened by car headlights flashing all around the bus. She listened to the high rpm whine of idling engines while lying in bed. Peering through the curtain, she saw bright headlights and a white van kept circling. What's going on, she thought? If it's cops, she wondered why they didn't just knock on the door and get it over with? She dreaded having to get up and be ordered to move on. She didn't want to have to drive around anymore tonight trying to find a place to be left alone, but the familiar engine sound was telling her it was a cop car. Why were they hovering and circling? Shadow wasn't barking so she decided to forget about it.

"If I have to deal with them, Lord, then you will help me," she whispered before drifting back to sleep.

Susan opened her eyes early the next morning and was ready to roll over and go back to sleep when suddenly she felt alarmed. Something was wrong. What was it, she wondered? She stared at the cracked windshield trying to figure out what was different when suddenly the fog in her brain cleared.

"The door is open!" she shouted. "Why is the door open?"

Susan sprang up and ran to the front of the bus. A cold chill having nothing to do with the early morning coolness came over her. Some of her clothing had been tied to the front door handle and left hanging from it. It was bizarre. She would never have done something like that, and the boys would have no reason to get any of her clothes out. But her mind was focusing on a problem of more serious consequence.

"Shadow is gone," she spoke to the silence in the bus. "Someone left the door unlocked and Shadow got out. Oh no!" she moaned. "Now I've got a stupid dog to find."

She glanced around outside in the immediate vicinity but couldn't spot the dog. "Shadow!" she yelled, disrupting the early morning stillness.

"Wait a minute," Susan struggled to remember. "I know I locked the front door. There is no way I would have forgotten, as scared as I am at night." She thought for a moment. That means someone from the inside had to have gotten up and let him out. Susan struggled with confusion.

"Kelly, did you go outside this morning?" she called sliding back the little door and peeking into Kelly's room. A soundly, sleeping boy snored in response.

No way that kid did it, Susan thought. Walking over to Caleb's room, she climbed up the ladder to see if he was the guilty party. "Caleb!" she hollered. Did you..."

But there was no Caleb. "Caleb!" she shouted again. "Where are you?" Susan ran to the bathroom to see if he was in there and quickly ran through the bus looking anywhere a small boy could hide. "Caleb, where are you?" she cried again.

Caleb was gone. Shadow was gone. The door was open. Looking through the windows, she still saw nothing. Somebody kidnapped Caleb, she thought as she stumbled down the stairs running outside. He never got up this early for any reason. She started screaming for Caleb and Shadow, running around to all the street corners and around nearby blocks. The panic grew as Susan became convinced someone had taken him, but why? And how did they get in? Susan ran to the pay phone a few yards from where the bus was parked and frantically called 911.

"My child is missing!" she shouted into the receiver trying to catch her breath. "My dog is gone, too! Somebody has taken my son! He was not in his bed this morning when I got up, and the door was open. I've been running around everywhere, and he is nowhere to be found." She felt like she would faint talking to the dispatcher.

"What was he wearing last?" the voice on the other end asked.

"I don't know. I don't remember. He was in bed, but he was wearing whatever he went to sleep in. I'm sorry. I can't think." She was trembling as she tried to cooperate with giving the description. "His name is Caleb, Caleb Dunn, and he is only five years old." Susan tried her best to answer the many questions. Tears were falling freely, but the terrified mother controlled her voice. "Why would somebody want to take a little boy? None of this makes sense."

"An officer will be right over," the lady assured her.

"I'm going to be looking right around here. I'm still hoping that for some crazy reason he will turn up, but I will stay close enough to see the officer when he arrives," Susan said before hanging up.

Next, she called Alan. The man at the public works who answered said it was too early for him to be at work but he should arrive momentarily.

More coins plunked in the machine and this time she called the Rescue Mission. "This is an emergency. Please tell Alan that Caleb is missing and I've searched everywhere," she told the man who answered. "Tell him I'm parked in the usual place."

"Hold on, ma'am. I don't think he's left for work yet."

On the phone, a shocked Alan said he would be right over. Because he worked for the Park's Department he took a few extra minutes to call the dispatcher, and they put a call out for all the city workers to search for the boy.

A black and white unit arrived immediately after Susan hung up. She ran to the car, breathless from running around the streets. "I've looked on all of these streets already," she informed. "Both dog and boy are nowhere to be found. He's never gotten up this early, but even if he had decided to take the dog for a walk or something strange like that he would never have gone out of sight. He's too afraid to do anything like that, so I know something bad must have happened."

The officer looked down at a sheet of paper he was holding. It looked like some kind of computer printout. "It says here that Caleb Dunn was picked up at Stearns Wharf last night at 1:30 AM and delivered to the police station. He was picked up by CPS and taken to an emergency foster placement."

Susan stared at the cop in total disbelief. "What the...?" her voice dropped off. "I don't understand. How can this be? Well, thank God he is okay!" She threw her head back, closing her eyes in relief. Her arms automatically rose into the air. "Praise the Lord! Thank you, Jesus! But how did this happen?" She rambled on with questions, shaking her head in denial.

"It says here that Animal Control was called and picked up the dog." He pointed at his printout. "It was taken to the County Facility at the same time. You can pick up the dog at this address, but there will be a small daily boarding fee to pay before you can recover him." The officer released a modicum of compassion when discussing the charge that would need to be paid to get the dog out of hock. He looked at Susan and his face brightened. "It's probably only about five dollars or so, and if you pick him up today that may be all you need."

The officer continued to deliver information devoid of emotion in a low monotone voice. "It says here to call CPS after 8:00 AM." He avoided looking at her, pointing to a yellow highlighted area on his sheet of paper. "Here's the person you need to talk to."

The flatline response to any questions regarding her child piqued Susan's curiosity. His lack of human reaction made her extremely uneasy, and she wondered how she had awakened into this surreal situation. The man sitting behind the steering wheel stared at the card with the phone number as he handed it over. She took it from his hands with questions running through her mind but knew this guy was not going to answer them. She no longer wished to talk to him. She only wanted to get her boy.

Alan arrived as the officer drove off. Kelly ran up to him and jumped in the car.

"You're not going to believe this, Alan. Wait 'til you hear," Susan said as she got into the front seat. Can I get a ride?"

"Sure," Alan replied. "I took the day off. Where are we going?"

The righteous person faces many troubles, but the Lord comes to the rescue each time.

Psalm 34:19 New Living Translation

Friends in High Places

Susan stared at the business card she had fished from her wallet. Virginia Scott, Child Protective Service, she read. They were on their way to the printed address a few miles away, but it was too early to call and she did not want to talk to the person the officer had given her.

"I can't believe what I'm hearing!" Alan was stupefied listening to her relate the previous evening's misadventures of her lost little boy. As he pulled into the parking lot of the Human Resources Department she thanked him for all of his help.

"We'll wait out here until you find out what to do next," he said. "You might be in there awhile. Don't worry about us."

The office had just opened, and Susan gave her little card to the receptionist. "I would like to speak to her if she is in and if it's possible."

It seemed like only a minute or two and Ms. Scott was standing at the door calling her name. A feeling of relief flooded through Susan as she followed quickly behind. It was a good beginning.

Once inside the tiny cubicle of an office, Susan poured out the story to Virginia as she knew it, admitting that she had no idea what really happened or how it had happened.

"So you found your clothes draped around the door handle and driver's seat?"

"Yes, but there were more of my clothes hung on other things around the bus. There is no reason to explain that.

Some were on the floor and stairs, and I know I didn't put them there. Also, the boys have never done anything like that before. They have never even wanted to get into my things. What worries me the most is that Caleb would never go outside alone. He has lots of fears and stays right near me no matter what."

"Was he upset the night before or days before?" The gray-haired matron assumed the role of a partner trying to assist in figuring out a mystery.

"He was a little bit the night before. He wanted me to come to bed and I always do when he asks, but last night I just wanted to stay outside and sing a little longer. The people at the City Hall were really enjoying it, and I felt so sorry for them. He didn't cry or carry on, nothing like that. It's just that it was out of the ordinary from the way I would do things. That could have upset him. But he didn't show it, and he did just as I asked him to do so I didn't think there was a problem. The little I can piece together about what happened is...well...my guess is if he were leaving the bus by any means then our dog, Shadow, would accompany him. He is a wonderful watch dog, and I am so glad it seems that he stayed with him. Did you know he had to have walked across Cabrillo to get to the pier? He was found out on the pier. Do you realize what could have happened if he had fallen off the pier? Oh my God! I can't believe this happened, but the report says it did."

Virginia nodded. "It sure is good it was the middle of the night. If a kid is going to cross that street at least at that time there wouldn't have been much traffic. It says here that a waitress from the restaurant was closing up and she found him sleeping on the bench at the end of the pier. She couldn't get close to him because the dog was barking anytime she tried to approach. It also says PD was called and upon arrival they couldn't get near the boy. The dog lunged and attacked if they made any move to get to him, so they backed off. He stayed asleep, and the dog quieted and remained vigilant by his side."

"Are you kidding me? See, I told you he was a good dog." Susan brushed the tears that were beginning to flow freely. "I always believed he would take care of Caleb, but I never expected anything like this would happen."

"Yeah, apparently the cops think so too. They left some comments that lead me to believe they were truly impressed with the dog." She continued reading from the computer printout. "It says Animal Control was called and arrived 1:20 AM, and the dog was taken into custody without incident. The boy was then taken into custody and questioned by officers, whereby he stated that his mother had left him there and he didn't know where she went. They made a search for his mother, but the bus was not in the area and could not be found. He was then taken to temporary foster care placement."

"What?" Susan squeaked. "What?" she repeated. That can't be true. He couldn't have said that. That never happened.

Virginia read it again. "That's what it says."

"I can't make any sense out of this. In the morning the bus was parked right where I was the previous night. It may have only been a parking lot away from the street and the pier, but anyone could see it was right where we always are. The police definitely know where we are. They drive by every night and sometimes several times. In fact..." Susan paused as though a dim bulb had grown brighter in her head. She looked up at Virginia. "In fact, they were there in the middle of the night. They knew exactly where I was.

They drove around and around the bus and then hovered for a long time. I had no idea Caleb or the dog was gone, and I didn't know the door was open, but they did. I wondered what was going on, and I waited for them to do something if they were going to, but then just went back to sleep. Why didn't they let me know? What was the reason for circling?"

Virginia shrugged and went back to the paper. "Would you like to talk to Caleb? I can let you call him if you would like? His case goes before the judge this morning, and it will be decided if he can be released or if he will be placed in foster care. You will know after 2:00 this afternoon. If I let you talk to him, you have to be very careful about what you say. Don't question him or direct him in any way. Just try and reassure him. That would be the best policy right now."

Susan was nodding yes while at the same time trying to process the full weight of what was happening. This was the moment in time when children were lost forever, and this was the county with a notorious reputation for doing just that. She thought she would get to pick up Caleb from wherever he was and then pick up her dog. She had been wrong. She could only get the dog. Guarding all of her reactions, she steeled herself to keep rising emotions under control. Calmly she said, "I would appreciate that so much."

Virginia dialed a number and talked briefly with the lady who answered. "He is up and around? Okay, well his mom would like to talk to him."

Susan took the phone and prayed for words. She wasn't sure of the rules, but she didn't want to lose a moment with this opportunity. "Caleb. Hi, honey. It's Mommy."

"Why did you leave me?" a tearful, angry, little boy on the other end of the line cried. "You left me! You drove the bus over to the pier and drove off without me."

"No, honey. I would never leave you. I didn't leave you."
Susan suddenly caught sight of Virginia scowling and
shaking her head. "I mean...I know you think I left you and I
know you are mad at me right now. All I can tell you is I
don't know what happened, but I promise you I will find
out. As soon as I find out, I will make sure it never happens
again because I love you, Caleb. You are my baby boy. I love
you so much. I would do anything for you."

Caleb was sobbing. "You left me," he wailed.

"Oh baby, I am so sorry. You must feel so afraid. I will get
you as soon as they say I can. Will you forgive me?"

"Yes," he cried. "I love you, Mommy."

Susan noticed Virginia motioning for the phone. "I love
you too, honey. I have to give the phone back now. I will see
you as soon as I can, okay?"

Virginia took the phone from her hand. Susan, stunned,
just shook her head slowly back and forth.

"He is convinced I left him. He believes I drove over to the
pier and just dropped him off and abandoned him. How
could he have that memory? It never happened! But he is
totally convinced and very upset. I can't figure this out no
matter what. Do you think he could have been
sleepwalking?"

Virginia looked sharply at Susan. "Has he ever sleep
walked before?"

"No, absolutely not. Not ever. None of my kids have. No
one I have ever known has, and I've only read about it. I just
can't think of anything that fits all of the pieces together. One
kid has had night terrors, but that isn't the same at all and
that happens to her infrequently."

Virginia went back to the paper and adjusted her glasses.
"It does say here that he was very sleepy and the social

worker was unable to get him awake to question him. His eyes remained bloodshot, he kept falling back to sleep, and they never felt they got him fully awake. It also says here that he was wearing some very unusual clothing that didn't fit and it was just kind of wrapped around him on top of some more appropriate jeans and t-shirt. He was barefoot."

Susan cheered up. "It does sound like sleepwalking, doesn't it? Have you ever heard of this happening before with kids? I mean it could happen and there would always have to be a first time."

"It kind of does," Virginia admitted. "Well, we are through here. Let me help you find your way back to the front. Like I said, you will know this afternoon so give us a call after 2:00 PM, and it is now up to the judge. I will put in my recommendation and that is all I can do."

"Thank you. At the very least I have a direction to go in to begin to figure this out. I don't know what will happen next, but I trust the Lord. I will do anything for Caleb. He is really hurting right now. All that matters is that he will be all right, and I am so glad that waitress found him when she did."

Susan left the building and saw Alan's white car parked in front.

"Are we getting Caleb?" he asked.

"No. We are getting the dog. We need to pray because I need a miracle to get Caleb. The good news is this will all be decided by 2:00 this afternoon. I will get him or I won't."

On the short drive to the animal shelter, Susan filled Alan in with all the details. She knew how slim the chances were but still hoped against hope that God would return her son. In the few minutes before getting the dog, she prayed silently but fervently. She vowed that she would do whatever was demanded by the ruling authorities to try to get him back and knew the minimal placement in foster care was six months. No, Lord, she thought. I need him back now because he needs me. Think about his needs, Lord. I am willing to accept whatever you do but please don't make Caleb suffer. We are a happy little family even if we are getting picked off one by one. We all love each other, and Caleb needs that kind of love to grow. I am believing for this afternoon. In Jesus name, Amen.

Shadow was glad to get back to his bus, and Susan continued to pray for Caleb's peace. The hands on the clock moved tortuously slow, and her anxiety increased the closer it got to 2:00. She grabbed her guitar and began to sing praises with all of her heart, songs of love to the One of love.

Like the last hour of the condemned before the execution, she felt the weight of the long walk ahead to the pay phone. "It's time," she announced. "Time to find out."

Alan was staring hard at her as she walked back from the phone, pale and nearly stumbling. "Well?" he asked.

"Let's go get Cabey," she smiled weakly.

"In prayer there is a connection between what God does and what you do. You can't get forgiveness from God, for instance, without also forgiving others. If you refuse to do your part, you cut yourself off from God's part.

Matthew 6:15 The Message Translation

Just Enough for a Bottle

Always a desert, Santa Barbara was caught in the grips of a severe drought. The townspeople desperately searched the skies for the long-awaited rain. Small business owners valiantly hung on to one more day, hoping to last a little longer for the rescue they knew could come with the change of weather. It was not to happen. A steady procession of defeated die-hards trickled out in overladen U-Hauls from the same road that had once carried them to the land of promise and opportunity. Those who remained were seen frequently glancing up at the sky hoping for a possible cloud.

Susan looked to the sky too. She looked to see if there was any need to worry about the leaky roof and kept praying about what to do. She checked out books from the library and studied roof building, researched different types of roof materials and choices of roof fastenings, and calculated building supply costs. It was overwhelming. Gathering information hadn't simplified anything. It only served to make her feel more inferior, and the problem of how to fix a roof grew larger in her mind.

As the entire town prayed for rain, she prayed, "Lord, you said Elijah was a human just like us, but he prayed that it would not rain, and it didn't for three years. I just want it not to rain until I can get the roof fixed, okay? No rain seems to be solving my problem, but is there anyone out there you could maybe send along to advise how to get this thing fixed?" With everyone she met, she made sure to mention,

"It leaks like a sieve." So far that remark had only produced chuckles. And so it was with great irony that the drought had been a tremendous relief to the stress of her worry while others were crushed from its effects.

Before the drought, Susan was exceptionally frugal with the water supply. Two five-gallon Sparklett's bottles could last a week. She would get the water at the Goleta church on Sunday and often made it just fine until the next time the faithful met. Friends from the church had blessed her with new used tires and a free YMCA gym membership, so showers were available to the family as long as she had gas to drive. No, water was never wasted at the bus. There were times, however, when things didn't go as well, and water was a hard thing to predict. One of those times caught her in a desperate situation.

The city had gone into survival mode and had been cracking down on everyone. They were forced to monitor shower usage in hotels, meters were put in public facilities, and residences were forbidden to water lawns. It got so bad that the police would issue citations if they caught anyone watering their lawn, and they were now being called the water police. People resorted to having their dead lawns spray-painted green. The mayor had proposed a desalinization plant to take ocean water and turn it into clean water. It would take a lot of money and quite a bit of time to build, but it would be a plan of protection for the future. The situation was indeed dire.

The Rescue Mission had been informed they were also going to have their water monitored. This caused a severe strain on the ones whose responsibility it was to meet the needs of the nightly unwashed homeless men, along with the men who were part of their drug rehab program. The mission had been doing the same as everyone else in the city by voluntarily finding ways to conserve. They had done their best for the good of everyone, but it would not suffice. The time had come for drastic measures.

Susan was aware of all of this, but Caleb decided to pick this time to get sick. It was a rare occurrence and an even more rare occurrence when her water supply suddenly ran out. Just as he spiked a high fever, he chose that moment to throw up all over his mother and the bed. She sparingly cleaned up the best she could and wiped him down. Throwing a worried glance at the emptying bottle, she realized she would need water to get him through the night.

"Caleb, we have to cool you down." Stripping off his shirt and jeans and rolling up the clothes in the dirty blanket, she tossed it into a plastic bag and walked it back to the laundry box.

"No, Mom," he protested. "I'm cold. I need my cwoze." He lie there shivering and whimpering. "Pweese, I need my cwoze."

"Caleb, you are sick. You have a fever and you are burning hot. We have to get your fever down and put water in you. I want to keep you in shorts until you are a little better." Susan grabbed a water bottle and put it to his lips. "Drink this, Caleb, and it will make the fever go away."

Shivering, he took a sip. "Cold, Mom. I'm cold," he cried.

Jackie stuck her head out of her cubicle. "Mom, is he going to be all right?"

"Yes, hon. This is not good, but I have dealt with a few fevers before. Don't worry."

Just then the front door of the bus rattled. It was Alan. "Hey, what's the matter with the Caleb?" he asked cheerfully. None of the usual whoops and hollers came from the little shivering lump in the back, but Kelly had burst from his room and leaped onto Alan from behind.

"Ugh! You got me!" Alan feigned surprise.

"Alan, I'm glad to see you. Got a sick kid here. He's spiking a fever, and I am out of water. Will you stay with him a minute while I go inside and get a bottle filled? I'll just ask for a little bit to get us through 'til the morning."

Alan put his arms out and smiled at the blubbering boy. Caleb crawled over into Alan's lap as Susan grabbed a 16 oz. water bottle on the counter. Uneasy about the fact she had allowed things to get this precarious, there was a certain foreboding making her feel insecure about approaching the woman in charge to ask for the water. Susan shrugged it away. I just feel bad because I hate to ask anyone for anything, she thought. I hate to have to depend on anyone other than myself.

Walking past the crowds of men standing around in the patio courtyard, Susan knocked at the front doors of the mission. A guard opened it to her.

"Can I speak to the boss for a moment?" she asked. "I need to get a little water." She held up the bottle.

"Sure," the man answered. "I think she's in her office."

Walking through the entry and past the kitchen, Susan found the lady she had come to know as her friend. She was sitting behind her desk in the small adjoining office, her black frame glasses low on the bridge of her nose as she looked over paperwork, and she glanced up at the approaching visitor.

"Hi. Sorry to bother you, but Caleb is real sick. He just spiked a high fever, and I ran out of water. I wondered if I could just fill a bottle until tomorrow. I don't want to be without through the night, especially if he is going to be sick."

Susan never expected a rejection. She didn't expect a lecture. She certainly wasn't without compassion for the difficult plight the woman on the other side of the desk was facing. Susan had thought she was talking with just another woman, another mother, someone who had shown nothing but kindness to both Susan and her boys. Most of all, Susan believed she had come to ask help from another Christian. But tonight, Susan was a homeless woman, and as such was not subject to the type of clients that this mission was required to utilize its water ration to serve. She was not in the group of those who could expect to ask for water, not even a bottle, not even for a sick child.

Susan only heard pieces of the lecture as the lady endlessly dragged on and on and in a stern tone about how terrible this was for her.

"They will close us down. You don't understand what we have to do here. Everyone expects us to take care, and we do the best we can. I can't permit any extra water use, not even a bottle. We have helped you a lot and we are not without compassion, but..."

"Just a bottle. I won't make a habit of this. My son has a fever," Susan repeated stupidly, recoiling from the sting of the lecture. Mentally, she vowed never to ask anyone here for anything again, not ever. She struggled to find a way to excuse the lecture, the stinging rejection, but rage and shame boiled inside. She was losing the forgiveness battle. It would come later but this was a scary night in a mean world, and she was being informed by the invisible enemy of her soul what a terrible mother she was. Every parent who has been unable to protect their child from pain, accidents, or sickness has known the feeling. Her guilt was compounded by the social position she found herself relegated to and tonight it was precarious.

I have to get out of here, Susan thought. I have to get out of here now. She began to slowly step out of the office, moving past the still-talking administrator of the liquid gold.

"I can't allow this again." The lady restated to the retreating, homeless mother. "The city is going to shut us down, and I won't be able to do anything about all the ones we are supposed to take care of."

"I'm sorry," Susan mumbled. "I'm very sorry." But she wasn't. She was hurt and she was mad, and she couldn't get away fast enough.

"I have no one on earth to go to," she whispered through tears which were falling rapidly now that she had escaped to the outside. "There is no one on this planet I can call except for you, Lord." Grabbing big gulps of air, she fought for control. Susan didn't want anyone to see her weak, didn't want them mocking and laughing behind her back. She swiped at her eyes quickly, opened them wide and forced back her feelings. The anger continued to grow, and she looked around to see if anyone might be watching her, then strode determinedly to the back of the building where an outside faucet was. A few men were standing around, and Susan boldly marched right up to it.

"Ed, I'm gonna fill this up real quick. Ran out of water, but I can get some in the morning. Cabey is sick."

Ed moved quickly out of the way and reached down to take the bottle from her hand. "Here, let me get that for you, little lady. Sorry to hear that. We will pray for him to get better right away. Sure love that little guy, both your little guys."

"Thanks, Ed. Yes, I need prayer. Thanks for everything." The heat of the anger began to melt. She hoped she was hiding everything well. They didn't seem to realize anything was different other than maybe a mom being worried about a sick child. Susan took the bottle, turned and rapidly made her way back to the bus. She wished she had never gone inside and asked for anything. The kindness of the men was soothing and comforting, but her feet took off running as soon as she was around the corner of the building.

"I can't believe what just happened, Alan!" Susan shouted, storming into the bus. "She didn't want me to get any water, not even a bottle. I am so upset! She is a mom. She is a Christian, and I thought she was a friend, but apparently we only had a professional relationship. I forget I am a client." Susan hid her face, fighting back the tears. Tears were not allowed. They were a luxury she could not afford.

"Jesus," she whispered. "Help me! Gotta hold it together. I got the water. I got the water. Thanks. I just needed a little bit. We'll be all right. We're gonna be okay." Silently Susan prayed. No one knows but you, Lord. I am so afraid, but right now no one knows that. I pray for my sister, Lord. She is a Christian. I can't figure out what is going on, but she is a Christian, and I pray for you to help her. I don't ever want her to find out how hurt I am. I don't want anyone to speak badly of the name of Christ because of this."

Susan glanced over to see Alan reach down and grab one of the empty Sparklett's jugs. She wondered where he was going to go to find water, guessing that was his plan. She watched through the window as he marched quickly toward the building she'd just left.

"Oh no! What does he think he is doing?" she cried. She ran out after him, but he was too fast for her to catch. When she rounded the corner to the back faucet, he was already filling up. Not knowing what to do, she just stood there and watched. Oh no! Oh no! What is going to happen? Frantically, she tried to think of words to use in her defense.

Alan, white-faced and determined, grabbed the full bottle and put it on his shoulder. He stormed off defiantly, walking back the way he came. Susan met him at the corner of the building.

"Alan, I'm going to get in lots of trouble." She kept her voice low so no one could hear. "They said we can't get water."

"To heck with that!" he shouted. "That's ridiculous! They get lots of money to help the homeless, and that's what you are. They can help some kids and their mom. Do you know how much money they got to build their new mission? I do! I'm not worried about this bottle of water. Anyways, if anyone dares to say anything you had nothing to do with it. I got the water!"

Back inside, Susan ran to check on a now sleeping, feverish boy who had crawled under blankets to deal with the chills. Pulling them off again, she grabbed a towel and dampened it.

Alan placed the bottle under the sink and spun around to leave. "Are you guys going to be all right now? If so, I'm taking off. I got to get up early tomorrow."

"Thanks, Alan. We'll be fine. I can take care of him. Kelly is asleep, and we're not going anywhere." Returning to the job at hand, she started to rub a hot little back and neck with the wet towel.

Caleb moaned, "Stop. Mom, stop."

"Only a little while, honey," she said soothingly, grabbing a newspaper to fan his dampened head and back. She didn't stop. It was going to be a long night, and there would be lots of time to think. There would be lots of time to pray. Healing would come.

"You got me through a doozy, Lord! But you got me

through." Anger was gone, shame was leaving, and fear was subsiding. It was giving way to quiet thanksgiving and praise for water, just for water.

"But everyone who will give you only a cup of water to drink in the name that you are one who belongs to The Messiah, amen, I say to you, he shall not lose his reward."

Mark 9:41 Aramaic Bible in Plain English

Receiving the Blessing

The weathered, old face smiled behind a scruffy, gray beard. His matted, long hair had been partially stuffed under a tattered, floppy-brimmed hat. The torn, blue, flannel shirt that hung from him testified of the many months spent crawling around and sleeping in bushes. Dirt clung in all the wrinkled creases and on every part of his exposed skin. The old man walked hunched over and grimaced with rheumatism and age. As he approached, Susan paused from her walk along the beach and turned her attention away from where Kelly and Caleb were shouting and splashing each other at the water's edge. She focused intently on the face in front of her, a face that told a story of long hours spent outside without shelter.

"Hi, there. My name's Leprechaun," he announced shyly. "My real name is Ray, but you can call me Leprechaun." He looked nervous and stared off into the distance. "Everyone else does. That's my street name."

"Okay, Leprechaun," she answered, slowly holding out her hand. "Nice to meet you." Susan could see bread crumbs and pieces of food stuck in the man's beard.

His eyes dropped and he stared at his feet. Susan reached over and grabbed his hand to shake it.

"I'm Susan. That's my street name." She smiled, but her feeble attempt at humor went unnoticed.

Leprechaun nodded politely. His head hung down as he spoke. "I saw your bus. I heard about what happened to you. I feel real bad for you and your poor little kids," he said

239

glancing over at the two small boys romping in and out of the surf.

Those poor little kids were at the moment a couple of playful pups, whooping and bursting with the sheer joy of being alive. Kelly pumped his little legs up and down, trying to leap in and out of the shallow water, his towhead bouncing while the sparkling green waves crashed around him. His brother squealed behind him.

"Wait, Kellwie. Wait!" His shorter legs wouldn't allow him to leap out of the water, but he laughed and jumped the best he could, trying to copy his leader.

Leprechaun cleared his throat. "It don't matter what they do to an old guy like me, but they shouldn't treat innocent kids like that." After a short pause, he added, "...and mothers. That's just not right." The old fellow looked stern and serious.

Susan looked down at the sand at her feet, thinking how to answer. "Well, yeah...uh...it was rough," she began hesitantly. "Nobody wants to see their loved ones suffer, but still the Lord takes care of us well." She looked back at the weather, scarred face.

The old man grunted. He didn't seem so sure.

"We do have to put up with a little persecution now and then. The Bible promised us that." Susan waited for her words to sink in. "Just think about what they did to Him? How could any of us ever complain if God's own son wasn't spared?"

Leprechaun stared at her. "I'm not a religious man. I'm just an old ex-con. I did many years in prison, but I paid my debt to society and I don't bother nobody. I wouldn't hurt no one, so you don't have to worry about me." He searched Susan's face to see if this new revelation had caused any alarm.

Susan stared back at him unflinching and smiling.

Leprechaun continued, "I still say they are wrong to pick on a vulnerable family who isn't hurting anybody, but just doesn't have a lot of money. If I ever can help in any way just let me know. I wanted to meet you when I saw your bus, and then I heard your story in the paper.

"I'm honored to make your acquaintance, Leprechaun," Susan spoke graciously and with a half bow as though she had just been introduced to the Prince of Wales. "Tell me something. Do you ever stay in the mission? Do you get enough to eat? I can tell you are outside a great deal of the time."

Leprechaun flushed. "No, no, I stay away from everybody. I don't bother anyone. I take care of myself just fine. I have a camp not too far away from here, and I do pretty good. It's hard to get up so early, but those of us who live in the bushes knows the rules. I don't need no one, you see." He shook his head emphatically. "I will watch out for your family." He turned and began to shuffle off down the beach. Looking back he called out over his shoulder. "If I can help I will."

"Thank you, sir. I appreciate that," Susan called out after him.

He seemed almost embarrassed as he made his way, and she had the feeling that he wanted to disappear and hide the shame of his existence. Even children recognize the telltale mannerisms of one who believes they are insignificant, one who wouldn't think of making a request for any need they had, genuine or not. Susan, herself, was well acquainted with these feelings, having lived with them most of her early life. Ingrained in her was a strong desire not to bother anyone, not to make waves. After many years, little had changed. She could, however, become instantly motivated on behalf of someone else.

In the following weeks, Leprechaun was frequently spotted dumpster diving or walking along the beach and always seemed surprised when one of the family would run up and greet him as an old friend. Susan would ask him if he needed anything and if he was all right. Leprechaun turned red with embarrassment every time with this attention.

"Do you have a Bible?" she asked one day while they stood around one of the stone, cylinder, trash receptacles placed along the bike path running parallel to the beach. She was feeling a desperation to reach this old man who "didn't want to bother nobody".

He reached into his shirt pocket and slowly pulled out a small New Testament he kept tucked inside. Susan and Leprechaun exchanged knowing looks. No words were necessary.

"You know you are very special to Him," she said finally.

Leprechaun looked away and his mouth began to frame words, but no sound came. He shook his head. "I don't know about that."

"If He had to strand me and my family on this beach just to give you that message, He would do something like that," she said, steadily watching the man in front of her. "Christians are expendable you know. We don't belong to this world anyway, though we still live in it, and our future is taken care of. Earth doesn't have anything more to offer. Besides, we're supposed to be bringing good news to everyone. And I believe we're supposed to be reminding His kids that they are valuable to the kingdom."

Leprechaun stood shaking his head, unsure.

"I think it's an honor to be sacrificed for that reason if that's what this is all for," she added. You are worth everything I am going through as far as I'm concerned. It's a privilege to be here, Ray." Susan turned and walked slowly toward her bus.

She didn't look back until stepping into her home on wheels to go inside. There he stood, blinking in the sun. He slowly turned and walked back toward East Beach, back to his home in the rocks and crags by the sea, back to his solitude and little pocket testament someone had given along the way.

In Santa Barbara during the 80's there was the inconvenience of something called the four-minute light on U.S. Highway 101. It was the only place in Southern California where everyone crossing the state was brought to a screeching halt with a set of stop lights at one small section of freeway. Quite a novelty really, unless you were sitting at this light waiting to go down to the beach and you couldn't make it across during the extremely brief time the majority on the highway found themselves momentarily detained. Perhaps those few seconds did cause some travelers to pause and turn off into the business district of town to deposit a few dollars, but mostly it was an annoyance to everyone.

Locals understood how important it was to get across as soon as possible, and this was a place and a time where drag racing was heartily encouraged. Engines raced as cars flew across the intersection at top speed. It was the only neighborly thing to do, allowing as many as possible to take advantage of the green light moment.

The day was gray and overcast, not a good one for tourists wanting to catch some rays. It was a rare time that the bus was the only one lined up at the four-minute light. Susan left the beach and was preparing to get back into town to meet the girls and pick them up from school before heading to the library. She felt lucky to be first at the light, and it was guaranteed that she'd make it across the first time without having to feel guilty for the slow lumbering turtle that had to be navigated across the freeway. Top speed was...well, let's just say it was most disappointing to those who were behind, gunning their engines and waiting.

"Mom!" shouted Kelly. "Wait! Don't go yet!"

"Wha...what's going on, Kelly?" His mom half-turned in her seat, straining to see what was causing the commotion. Her son was upstairs looking out of the rear window.

He bounded down the ladder from the bedroom loft and raced toward her. "Mom, it's Leprechaun! He's running and yelling at us to wait!" Kelly looked wild-eyed at his mother. "What do you think is wrong?"

No one in the family had ever seen the old man yell or run before. They had never even seen him get excited. Susan looked into the rear view mirror, trying to see what he was holding up. It looked like a small white bag, and he was hollering for them to stop. She reached over and pulled the lever, opening the bus door, and motioned with her head for Kelly to jump outside and get a better idea of what was happening. She glanced back making sure no cars were behind.

A few blocks back, the old guy continued to run in a race against time. "Wait!" yelled the energized Leprechaun. "Wait! Take this. Hurry!"

"Mom, I think he wants to give us something, but we're gonna miss the light!" Kelly yelled from the street.

A sudden realization occurred to Susan. Leprechaun had been dumpster diving, and he'd found some prize amidst the trash. He was desperate to get it to the family to share and knew the four minute light would take them away until the next day. Maybe he had never behaved in this way before, but she knew the gift could not be refused.

"Run, Kelly! Run as fast as you can so he won't have to. Get it from him and tell him thank you very much. We have to take his gift, no matter what!" Susan yelled. "I don't care what it is! Hurry!"

She thought to herself if we miss the light, then we miss the light. No problem, Lord. Her hands beat nervously against the steering wheel as she watched the small boy racing toward the man, who at this time was close enough for her to see his bright red face. He looked like he could have a heart attack or a stroke. She pushed her hand out of the window in a wave.

"Thank you!" she yelled at the top of her voice. Susan thought he probably couldn't hear, but when she looked out from the mirror she could see him smiling and waving.

Kelly snatched the treasure and turned to run lickety-split back. Looking straight ahead at the changing light, he raced like an Olympic medalist in a final sprint to the finish line. Susan slowly started moving the bus forward, and Kelly hopped on board in a final effort just as the light was turning yellow. His mother gunned the engine, and everyone inside cheered as they raced across.

"Yeah! We made it!" they shouted. Susan pulled over once they were on the other side. They all hopped out and waved at an uncommonly jubilant Leprechaun. He turned and disappeared, and they stood there looking at each other.

"It's sugar!" exclaimed Kelly and Caleb, both now staring at what Kelly held in his hand. It was only a bag of sugar. There was a rip on the top, but the bag was overall in fairly good shape.

"Yes, it is sugar," said their mother. "Let's get back inside. Her demeanor changed from celebratory to serious when she reached over and took the prize from Kelly's hand. "And I never, never, never want you to tell anyone we threw it away. Do you understand me?" She gave the boys a rare "better never ever" look, and they nodded at her looking equally serious. Once inside, she dumped the precious substance into the trash can under the sink.

"Why, Mommy? Why?" wailed Caleb, suddenly upset. Dat's good shuga. I can put it on my ceweal. Why you fwowing it away?"

"Cabey, it came from the trash. We don't know if it's okay. Maybe it is, but we can't take a chance. You could get very sick." She looked down at a little boy who trusted her implicitly but was obviously struggling to make sense of her actions. "But we also can never tell Leprechaun that we threw his gift away. That would be the same to him as if we threw him away. Do you understand?"

Kelly nodded his head. Caleb was still confused. "But why did you make Kelwie wun to get the shuga so we could just fwow it away?" Caleb shrugged his shoulders and put his hands up.

"Because," Susan explained, "Leprechaun needed to give his love to us."

Caleb stared forlornly at the sack sitting in the trash. "I still think it's good."

"Caleb, we have sugar already, lots of it. Mom will buy more if we need it. Kelly was losing patience with his brother. "Don't worry about it."

"We wuv Wepwechaun, Mom." Caleb looked up at his mother. "He doesn't have to give us anything."

"No, Caleb. He doesn't, but..." his mother added, "this is a very special day. Even though I threw it away, I will never forget this bag of sugar.

Susan leaned down and grabbed both boys in a big hug as wave after wave of joy poured over her. "I am starting to believe there are many adventures just beginning for us. God wants to use us for some strange reason in this place even though we are the most unimportant nobodies of all the nobodies. I am nothing more than a mom blessed with some of the best kids who ever existed. There is no way we could withstand all of the things that have been coming against us, yet we remain. We aren't being destroyed. Instead, we're thriving. I don't know how God does this stuff."

She looked down at two happy faces. "You know, guys, I love this feeling. It seems to be growing more each day. For the first time in my life, I feel like I belong. Yes, I finally found where I belong."

If you made it this far, would you consider writing a review?

https://www.amazon.com/author/susandunncobb.

Thank you.

Epilogue

Though we walk through paradise where treasures abound,
Fret not for the ones who stay on the ground.
Some pearls stay hidden and stuck in their shells,
Souls who're struggling in their own private hells.

The darkness surrounding keeps love away,
But wherever there's light, the darkness can't stay.
Hold onto the gift placed in your hand,
Grab your candle, and light up the land.

Never believe your light is too small
Or that it won't do any good at all.
And as you watch that flame burn away
The blind will be able to find their way.

The deaf will hear the sound of their cry.
The prisoners will run from chains that now lie
Broken and empty of those once held bound,
Those that chose freedom when freedom was found.

Hold high your candle as long as it burns.
So many will thank you when Jesus returns,
For sharing His love is why we are here.
The truth of His Word makes everything clear.

www.ingramcontent.com/pod-product-compliance
Lightning Source LLC
Chambersburg PA
CBHW060242290526
45789CB00001B/159